A Choice Theory Approach

To

Drug and Alcohol Abuse

By

Michael Rice, LISAC, RTC

ii

A Choice Theory Approach to Drug and Alcohol Abuse

Copyright 2009 by Madeira Publishing Company

Madeira books may be ordered through booksellers or by contacting:

Madeira Publishing Company
1550 E. University Dr, Suite J-1
Mesa, AZ 85203
480/898-3015
http://www.madeirapublishing.com

Author's photograph taken by Drurygene Boelter
Cover photo and design by Lynn K. Busby

ISBN: 1449501079
EAN-13 is 9781449501075.

Table of Contents

Endorsement

Choice Theory®, developed by William Glasser, M.D. provides a simple, yet profound explanation of human behavior. As a psychiatrist that practiced for 50 years working with all kinds of patients and diagnosis, he has recently stated that all he has ever really been is a teacher; a psychiatrist that teaches people to be happy.

A Choice Theory Approach to Drug and Alcohol Abuse is a continuation of Dr. Glasser's theory and teachings. Mike Rice teaches people how to be happier.

One of the easiest to understand principles is also one of the most difficult lessons to practice; "The only person you can control is yourself." Mike explains that even though people logically agree with the statement, many people spend their time trying to change others through the use of negative or "deadly" habits. These behaviors hinder relationships and increase unhappiness.

Mike will teach you some new ideas, show you different ways of looking at the problem of addiction, and will provide information you need to help you move toward happiness. The logical progression of ideas, coupled with explanations, case studies, and opportunities for self-reflection, make this a powerful, effective tool for anyone wanting help with an addiction.

Bob Hoglund, Bob Hoglund, Inc.
Senior faculty Member of the William Glasser Institute

Acknowledgements

This book is the result of having put the works of Dr. William Glasser, M.D. into a definable and practical method in treating addictions. I have been using the principles in Reality Therapy and Choice Theory in my own life as well as my working with clients for the last 8 years. Prior to incorporating Choice Theory into my private practice, I had been utilizing Albert Ellis's Rational Emotive Therapy. It wasn't until Dr. Glasser saw the need that we, as a civilization, need a new psychiatry that can easily be understood by all that I was able to notice tremendous headway in working with my clients.

Also involved in this work are the hours of editing, suggestions, comments, and corrections contributed by Lynn Busby. I find it difficult enough to maintain my private practice and write without having to edit and correct. Her assistance, along with that of my office manager, Sheena Sattarpour has been invaluable.

My greatest teachers have always been my clients. Over the years, they have continued to show me what works and what doesn't work.

Foreword

If you have issues with addiction or live with an addict, you have just picked up a book that could transform your life. This is a book I'll be recommending to my trainees, colleagues and clients as an immensely practical and helpful book.

There is no jargon, or complicated theory. Michael has combined his skills and experience with a highly effective therapeutic approach, incorporating the practice of Reality Therapy with the underlying principles of Choice Theory. This book is not an intellectual, theoretical exercise, but is grounded in the day to day practice of a drug and alcohol therapist. It is written as a direct result of personal and professional experience combined with a theoretical framework (Choice Theory) that works.

Gary Cziko in his book 'Without Miracles' writes, "Choice Theory does what no behaviorist stimulus response theory has ever been able to do – it provides an explicit working model that accounts for goal oriented purposeful behavior."

This model provides powerful leverage for assisting people to manage their lives more effectively.

Michael uses an easy to read, conversational style, sprinkled with real case studies, which are direct and hard hitting. He makes extensive use of the Reality Therapy process through evaluative questioning, avoidance of judgment and the presentation of information about drug use, its effects and the process of recovery from addiction.

Michael emphasizes the Choice Theory / Reality Therapy axiom that good relationships and self evaluation are the path to happiness and sobriety. His book goes far beyond simple behavioral recommendations to the underlying causes, specifically the poor relationships in our lives which are the result of an external control belief system. His focus is always on how we can move to higher levels of authenticity, wellbeing and happiness, and how simply ceasing dependence on an addictive substance will not bring us happiness.

This book reflects honesty, directness, skill and extensive personal and professional experience. I first met Michael during a training program with the William Glasser Institute. His presentation on Drug and Alcohol Abuse was the clearest and most helpful I had heard. Furthermore, observing Michael role play using the ideas and approaches described in his book, it became clear that he "walks his talk", and has the integrity and skill to put these ideas into practice.

We are part of a society which does not deal well with drug and alcohol addiction. These ways of dealing with unhappiness cost our society billions of dollars annually, result in huge productivity losses, and destroy the lives of addicts and those who live with them. Because Michael sees himself as a teacher of happiness, he is able to focus not only on the practical steps required to assist the addict, but on the underlying causes, and hence explain how we can manage addiction in a holistic way.

 Enjoy this book.

Ivan Honey, Psychologist
Senior Faculty William Glasser Institute

Preface

One of the most common threads addicts and alcoholics have is that they don't want anyone telling them that they have a drug or alcohol problem and ways to overcome their addictions. In fact, most of them feel that their situation is so unlike any another addict's or alcoholic's situation that no one else could possibly understand their situation.

I can't make anyone stop drugging or drinking but I can give addicts the tools for them to do it themselves. Let's face it. If the addict or alcoholic knew how to stop their alcohol or drug dependence, they would have done it a long time ago. "I just wanna do it my way." Translation: "Keep your opinion to yourself. I'm not as bad off as you think I am. I won't see any psychiatrist 'cause I'm not crazy. You can't get me to ever go to A.A. and that God thing. No one really understands my problems except me. I'll stop when I'm good and ready. I'm not ready."

This book is designed to be a practical, easy read on the topic of addition recovery. During my years of practice as a behavior therapist focusing on drug and alcohol addiction, I have been able to see people successfully turn their life around using the methods described in this book. I didn't do it or make them change. They were all able to do it themselves once they were shown how to develop the tools. They found new ways to do it themselves.

I hope to be able to leverage the success I have witnessed in my practice by sharing the knowledge I have gained from Dr. William Glasser and applying it to the world of substance dependence.

x

None of the people whose stories I relate to in this book have been identified by their real names for obvious reasons. Their stories are real, their names are not.

My elevator speech is simply, "I teach happiness."

All those open to learning a new way to live life; to forsake the "pleasure" of substance abuse for real happiness, read on.

Who Will Read This Book

Right now, I would be willing to bet that you are thinking, "Alcoholics and addicts will be reading this book." Am I right? Actually, addicts and alcoholics will be the lowest number of individuals reading this book. After all, in their minds, they don't believe they have a problem with drugs or alcohol so why would they even pick up such a book?

The majority of readers will be those of you who live with, love, have a family member or friend who is an addict or an alcoholic. Your first thought is that if you can glean some knowledge about addiction, you will be able to help (another word for "change") the person in your life who has an addiction problem. The next group of people who may read this book will be those who work in the field of recovery from addiction.

Then, after those of you who do finish this book, some of you will be tempted, and others will be more direct, to give this book to the addicted person in your life. The addicted person will most likely look at the cover, tell you that *you* are the one who needs help, and throw the book across the room or in the trash. A few of them will come back, when you aren't looking, and pick it up and begin to read. They will do so when it becomes their idea to read it and not because you wanted them to read it.

The book is actually written for anyone who is addicted to drugs/alcohol and anyone who is involved with someone who is addicted to drugs/alcohol.

So, before I even begin, I want you to know: I can not make anyone stop drinking or using drugs. If I had that kind of power, I would be on Oprah's show tomorrow morning. I can't control anyone but myself and you can not control anyone but yourself. This does not mean that there is no hope for the recovery from addiction. On the contrary, you have several choices for help.

Inside this book, you will find some very effective means of getting your life back, whether or not you are the alcoholic/addict or the victim of one. Even if you aren't affiliated with any substance abuse, you will find some important information. The information consists of life enhancing principles as well as teaching you new ways to deal with life on life's terms, not *your* terms. If your terms were effective, you would not need to read this book. You would not be addicted to any substance. Your life would be fairly stress-free. You would have little, if any, conflict with anyone in your life. And if you did have conflict, you would know how to deal with it before it would escalate. You would not be experiencing any aches and pains of which you are attributing to being out of shape or merely getting older. If your ways of dealing with life were effective, you would be happier than you have ever been. You would have meaningful relationships. You would have all of your basic needs of Survival, Love, Power, Freedom, and Fun met. You would be enjoying more of your potential than you thought possible.

This is a different approach to dealing with alcohol and drug dependence mixed with some of the more traditional methods. This approach is centered on learning who and what you can control, understanding why you do anything that you do, and finding happiness through meaningful relationships with the important people in your life.

Pre-Treating the Addiction Problem

Before we can get started in dealing with addictions, a crash course in Reality Therapy and Choice Theory will be necessary. For you to be effective in your effort in dealing with addiction, whether you are the addict or the person who loves the alcoholic, this information is the key to your success in reaching your desired results.

There are many different ways of dealing with addiction. If you have tried one or several ways and have not been successful, this may be just what you needed. No program will work if you don't really want to make, or see a need to make, some changes in your life. If what you have been doing hasn't been working for you and there is a large gap between what you want and what you have, this program is designed to look at and learn some different things that could get you the results you want.

Perhaps the most difficult task you must learn will be breaking the age-old beliefs that you are a victim of life and that others are responsible for your unhappiness . . . that you may be mourning the loss of a life you feel you should have had . . . that if others would do what you want them to do, you would be a happier person. Who can we control? If you answered, "only me," then you are half way there. Saying it and doing it are two different things. Just look at the above sentence at the middle of this paragraph a notice how the message is, 'if others would do what I want them to do, I would be happier.'

Since the only person we can control is ourselves, the best way to control the events in our life is through what we do and not what others do. When you begin to change some things that you do, others around you will automatically begin to change some things that they do and everyone will begin to feel better. Self-assessment is <u>essential</u> to improving your life rather than assessing other people in your life.

What's in it for you? How about happiness? Does peace of mind sound good if you happen to be someone who is involved with someone with an addiction problem? How about sobriety or a life free from drugs? Is that something you would like to have? Perhaps you might also want peace of mind, satisfying relationships, love, acceptance, respect, suitable income, freedom, and fun. You may even suffer from aches and pains which may subside once you learn Reality Therapy and Choice Theory. All you have to do is ask yourself, are any of these benefits the things that you would like to have?

The concepts of Choice Theory are simple and easy to use. They can also be taught to very young children. In fact, it may be easier to teach the younger children easier than adults because they have not been using all the old ways of behaving that have not been effective as long as some adults have.

You will learn:

- Who We Can Control
- Why We Are Unhappy
- Why We Behave the Way We Do
- Our Tool Kit to Solve Unhappiness
- Our Total Behavior
- How to Resolve Unhappiness
- And finally: How to Get Clean and Sober

Getting Clean and Sober is last on the list because the methods to get there will all be contained in the other 6 areas of knowledge and awareness. If you are someone who lives with or loves and addict/alcoholic, you will most likely follow the order and read this book from front to back. If you happen to be an addict or alcoholic, you will most likely go to the last chapter about How to Get Clean and Sober and skip all the other information.

To get to a place that you have never been before, you need a map or else you need someone who knows the way to take you there. The information beginning at the front of the book is your map as well as your guide to get you to being Clean and Sober.

Again I want to caution you, the reader, to read this book in order rather than jump around looking for a quick answer or fix to your particular situation. Addicts and alcoholics want recovery now! They don't want to have to wait for it. So when it comes to reading self-help books, they cut to the chase and don't read or learn all the preliminaries they need to have to put it all together.

Many addicts and alcoholics tend to believe that they are not like other addicts or alcoholics . . . that they are different and don't fit the profile of your standard addict or alcoholic. If that were the case, the most effective way of treating addiction, Alcoholics Anonymous (A.A.) and group therapy, would not exist. A.A. has been around for over 72 years and still going strong. Group therapy sessions are successful because the members eventually realize that they have more in common with one another than they thought. All addicts and alcoholics have two things in common right off the bat: shame and guilt. This will be addressed later.

The next thing an addict or alcoholic wants to know before giving up on substance reliance is: "What's in it for me?"

To answer this question, I will need to ask you some other questions so that you can see what may be missing in your life that you are compensating for with drugs or alcohol.

What are those things in your life that bring you happiness? (You can bet that alcohol or drugs are one of them at this stage).

What are those things in your life that you want but don't have?

Who in your life is behaving in a way that you disapprove of? (Did you include yourself on the list?)

Has what you have been doing brought you any closer to those important things in your life or have they pushed you farther from them?

If you could answer the first three questions without any difficulty, you most likely have a pretty good idea of what it is in your life that makes you happy. If, however, your response to the last question was "no," then *that* would be your payoff . . . learning new methods to get your needs met.

So if what you want in your life is happiness, sufficient or more than sufficient income, love, respect, freedom, and fun, then buckle your seatbelt and let's have some fun learning some new things.

Who Can We Control?

For the victim of an addict or alcoholic: When you get unhappy with any important person in your life that is addicted, you get to feel sick, tired, drained, angry, depressed, and helpless.

For the addicted person: When you are unhappy, you get to drink or do drugs. Now, who has the problem? The addict will most certainly say, "Not me. You all are the ones with the problem." And he'd be right. Any problem he may see in his life is taken care of with drugs or alcohol. In Choice Theory, we only control the things that we can control in our own lives and no one else. In A.A. we say that if it is something that is out of your control, "Let Go and Let God." Why worry and fret over something that you can do nothing about? You'll only choose to get upset, sick, or drink and/or use drugs. The Serenity Prayer that is often used in A.A. meetings says it all, "Grant me the serenity to accept the things I cannot change, the courage to change the things I can, and the wisdom to know the difference."

I ask my group members this question all of the time: Who can you control? Invariably, I always get the same answer: "Just our self." And yet, I have little doubt that you have been trying to control others throughout your entire life. So if you know that you can only control yourself, why even attempt to control someone else?

Dr. Glasser (1998) explains in his work that the world's psychology is something that he calls, "External Control." External control is used by all cultures and all people of the world. Dr. Glasses explains, "it is an 'I know what's better for you than you do' type of psychology that destroys all relationships with those who use it."

External control as explained by Dr. Glasser has the purpose of

1) Giving us an excuse to not have to take responsibility for our behavior. "If you hadn't done what you did, I wouldn't have done what I did."
2) External control gives me the power to get you to do something that you don't want to do and you can use it to get me to do what I don't want to do.
3) Once we learn what is right for us in our own life and our own world, we come to the conclusion that we also know what's right for everyone else as well. And once we begin to believe this, we begin to get into trouble with all of our relationships.

For the person who cares for the addict/alcoholic:

If you have tried to get the addict/alcoholic in your life free from addiction, how successful have you been? What worked? What you probably did was use all the controlling tools you have gathered over the years to get others to do what you want them to do. You resorted to what Dr. Glasser refers to as, The Seven Deadly Habits (1998) that you use on other people whenever you want them to do something that they don't want to do. Those seven habits of external control are:

- Criticizing
- Blaming
- Complaining
- Nagging
- Threatening
- Punishing
- Bribing or Rewarding to get someone to do something they don't want to do.

The seven deadly behaviors above are the things people do to try to control another person. And you said you could only control yourself. Why would you do those things if you can only control yourself? Do you ever do them to your best friends? I would venture to say that you don't. If so, they wouldn't be your friend for very long. So then why would you do any of them on those whom you love the most?

How effective are any of these behaviors when it comes to getting someone to do something they don't want to do? If you used them on your addict or alcoholic, they most likely drank or used even more. Meanwhile, either you are too stressed to eat or else you began eating more. You can't sleep or you sleep all the time. You've lost weight from worry. You worry night and day. You can't concentrate. You have aches and pains and may have been told by your doctor that you have fibromyalgia. The most common way people show their unhappiness is through aches and pains. Just look at all the things you are choosing to do out of frustration because you haven't been successful at controlling someone else.

Not only do none of the seven deadly habits work to bring you closer together, they will be very successful in destroying whatever you have left in a relationship with the person on whom you use them. Any one of these habits will destroy respect and with that will go any love that may exist. So if you want the addicted person in your life to quit their addiction, don't use the seven deadly habits. These habits will have the opposite effect of what you want them to do.

The only thing that you can do is whatever it is you can do for yourself and not another person. First of all, STOP any and all of the seven deadly habits. Secondly, find yourself an Al-Anon meeting and start attending. Look under "Alcohol" in the yellow pages.

Al-Anon is a support group for people who are married to or have someone in their life close to them that has an alcohol or drug problem. It consists of people who are in the same situation they are in and they support one another. Al-Anon is called "The Other Side of the Program" in A.A. Meetings can be found in your phone book under alcohol or under the central number for A.A. who would be able to direct you to the nearest meeting.

If you can't find "Al-Anon" find the Alcoholic Anonymous number and call them and ask them where the nearest Al-Anon meeting is in your area. The meetings are free and you'll find a lot of support from people who are in the same position as you. You can also contact their website:

http://www.al-anon.alateen.org/english.html

For The Addict/Alcoholic:

I just got a whole lot of people off your back for you. So now that they have quit complaining, you don't have to do whatever you've been doing to counteract *their* behavior. There's no need for you to lash back with your own use of the seven deadly habits.

Right now, you have the freedom to make your own choices. Do you really want to continue to go on with your life the way it has been? Do you think your addiction will just go away if you continue to simply ignore it? Addiction, especially alcoholism, is a progressive process. It gets worse before it ever gets better, unless you stop. Most will die before they ever get around to doing something about it. Since the only person you can control is yourself, you need to know the right tools to use in order to do that. So far, the only tools you have tried in order to stop have let you down. Don't feel badly. All the tools your friends and family have used to try to get you to stop have failed them too. The only thing either of you have succeeded in doing is using the seven deadly habits which has harmed your relationship with one another and love and respect you once had for one another has gone out the window.

Perhaps you haven't even tried to quit for any long term because you know what it feels like to not use or drink. The withdrawals you may have had felt worse than when you use or drink so you choose to use or drink to make them go away. Your drug is your temporary relief from withdrawal symptoms. Do you know what the symptoms of withdrawal are?

Depending on what drug you have been using or drinking, withdrawals come in many forms. Common symptoms are:

> Sweating
> Hallucinations (Audible or visual or both)
> Irritability/Anger
> Seizures
> Nausea
> Shakes or trembling of the hands and body
> Severe aches and pains throughout your body.
> Hot or cold flashes
> Vomiting
> Nightmares
> Dreams of using or drinking
> Severe craving for the drug.
> Poor concentration
> Diarrhea
> Memory lapses

The above symptoms are absolute proof that your body is addicted and dependent on a drug. Alcohol is a drug. The only difference is that it comes in liquid form. If you have been experiencing any of the above symptoms, you cannot deny that the drug has control of you rather than the other way around. You may even require medical detoxification from the drug if you are experiencing hallucinations, seizures, and trembling.

So here are your choices that you may not have tried yet:

• Have an alcohol/drug assessment made to see where you are with your use and what kind of treatment you need.

.• Go to A.A. or other support group such as Rational Recovery, SMART Recovery, hospital, or religious programs.

• Enroll in an outpatient alcohol/drug program which you will find in the yellow pages of your phone directory. (Typically under "Alcohol").

• Check into a Detox facility if necessary

• Check into an in-patient treatment program that offers intensive treatment and medications should they be needed to assist you in your withdrawals.

If you are like most addicts/alcoholics, you didn't even get past the first choice before your addicted brain jumped in and said, "I don't need any of that shit! I can do this on my own, without any help from anyone!" If that were true, you would have stopped a long time ago.

For many of you, the fact that you are still alive seems to be proof enough that you don't have a problem with drugs or alcohol. You have this belief system that says that all you have to do is stop, and right now, you don't want to stop. The reality of it is that you can't stop. If you could stop, you would have done so a long time ago before you began losing your family, your job, your relationships, your friends, your health, your spouse, your children, and your money. Soon, the only thing left to lose is your life.

A very popular saying in A.A. is that you must hit "rock bottom" before you will quit. The problem with that belief is that some people have a bottom so deep that they will die before they ever get to it.

Your ego is also telling you that there is no way that you are out of control. But if you cannot not drink, then you are not in control. Others think they can control their use with will power. The next time you have diarrhea, try to see how long you can control that with will power. You may pinch your sphincter muscles for a short time but eventually, they will give up and then you have two choices to make: Hope you can reach a toilet in time or get ready for an embarrassing need for a change of clothing.

I recently had a client who had received two DUI arrests in the last three years. His wife left him because of his drinking. He came to me to get a clearance by a licensed therapist go get his drivers' license reinstated. After completing an intake and assessment and giving him three standardized tests to evaluate his past, present, and future possibility of use, I asked him, 'has your drinking ever caused you any problems in your life?'

Not so surprising he answered, "No."

So then I asked him, 'has your drinking ever caused you any legal problems?'

He answered, "No."

'You got two DUI charges. Aren't those legal problems?'

"Well, if you put it like that, I guess it is."

'Has your drinking ever caused you financial problems?'

"No."

'How about all of those fines you have to pay?'

"Well, when you put it like that, I guess it does."

'Has your drinking ever caused you relationship problems with someone that you cared about?'

"No."

'Then why did you wife leave you?'

"OK. I guess my drinking has caused some problems. But it hasn't cost me my job and I still work harder than anyone else who doesn't drink."

The alcoholic's perception of his world and that of the real world are not in synch. This is why he continues to drink. If he doesn't perceive a problem due to his drinking, why would he even consider giving it up? As long as he has a job, he doesn't see any problems caused by his drinking.

Are you still not sure if you have a problem or not? Let's look at some of your behaviors.

Do you steal from your family, friends, or strangers to get money in order to buy your drugs?

How normal is that?

Do you spend most of your time thinking about, talking about, or procuring drugs or alcohol?

How normal is that?

Do you hide your alcohol so no one will know how often or how much you drink?

Do you hide your alcohol because someone would be upset if they knew you were drinking or using?

Do normal drinkers hide their drinking from others?

Do you lie about your drinking or using to your family or friends?

How normal is that?

Do you usually drink your first few drinks fairly fast or chug them down?

When was the last time you had 3 or more lemonades or teas in less than 15 or 20 minutes? Normal drinkers don't do that.

When was the last time you drank 12 or more soft drinks in a night? Normal drinkers don't do that.

Have you lost family or friends due to drinking/using or do they avoid you?

Have you lost any jobs because of drinking or using?

Does family or do your friends ever complain about your using or drinking? Do they complain about everyone's drinking/using or just yours?

Have you been arrested for any alcohol or drug related charges?

Do you feel sick if you don't drink or use?

Do you drink or use on the job with the possibility of being fired if caught?

Do you sneak off to take drugs when you are socializing or in a meeting?

Do you drink alone?

Do you take addictive pain medications for more than 6 weeks if you have been in pain?

Do you take addictive pain medications when you are not in pain at all?

Do you try and talk your doctor into giving you a refill on your scripts when they have run out too early?

Do you have several doctors that you use at different times to provide you with your addictive medications?

A "yes" response for any one of the above behaviors would indicate loss of control.

So what do you do? Let's begin by asking, what have you done so far that worked? If the answer to that is "nothing has worked so far," then you would benefit by finding other methods that may or may not work. You won't know unless you try, right? If I could show you how to get the life and happiness you would like to have, would you be willing to give it a shot?

Whether you believe this or not, as difficult as it is for some people, stopping the use of drugs or alcohol is the easy part. The hard part is staying off of drugs or alcohol. Abstinence is one thing, recovery is something totally different.

Karen, (not her real name) came to me because she had been arrested for DUI, her second offense. Karen was a very power driven person who was successful in her business life and one who believes that anyone can have what they want in life if they make the proper choices. She also carried around a lot of stress and uneasiness because she was a believer in control of her own life. She was not a drinker until she went on a cruise around the age of 40, and discovered that a glass of wine "made me feel wonderful. It was like the weight of the world was lifted from my shoulders." Consequently, she began to drink wine regularly in order to feel better and ease her stress.

While Karen had not crossed the line into biochemical addiction, she had developed the psychological addiction of using it to make her feel less stressed and to feel happier. After her first DUI, Karen went to her family doctor whom she had relied on for the last 22 years. She told him, "I have a drinking problem." Her doctor told her, "you don't have a drinking problem, you have a stress problem."

The doctor failed to look at Karen's behavior of consuming alcohol on a regular basis and as a means to deal with her emotions. He decided that she had a general stressful condition and the cause of her unhappiness was due to this stress. His remedy: Prescribe Effexor, an antidepressant also used for anxiety that will affect her brain's ability to do what it does that leads to her thoughts and subsequent stress. In the doctor's world, Karen's stress was due to anxiety so he decided to medicate her for anxiety.

Meanwhile, Karen continued to drink because the Effexor didn't do anywhere near as well as what alcohol did for her. Her doctor was only substituting one drug for another, thinking that the medical drug would take care of her stress better than alcohol. Of course, he was wrong. Nothing numbs emotions better than alcohol because it is instant relief. Medical drugs take time to be effective.

Karen's drug of Effexor is one that if taken for at least one week will require a doctor's supervised discontinuance due to possible serious withdrawals. To cease the use of Effexor, doses need to be shaved gradually over a period of time before one entirely stops taking it. And . . . it should never be taken with alcohol.

Karen's story doesn't end here. While she remained on the Effexor, she knew she still wanted to drink and that it was causing her problems which she could not control. Feeling out of control to someone who is a major controller in their own personal life is something Karen could not accept. So she looked up alcohol treatment in the phone book and checked herself into a hospital . . . another medical model of dealing with addiction.

Because Karen had checked into the hospital telling them, "I have an alcohol problem," she was immediately put into a seven day detox program without the benefit of even being diagnosed as to what degree her addiction might be. She was also given Valium to "ease her withdrawal symptoms." The purpose of a substance abuse assessment is to determine where or how far a person is with their substance abuse and then refer them for adequate treatment. The only thing worse than too much treatment is not enough treatment. The purpose of a substance abuse assessment is to determine what kind and how much treatment a client may need.

Karen was not assessed and evaluated. The hospital staff only heard, "I have an alcohol problem," and rushed her into detox. Had they assessed her, they would have found out that Karen was not biochemically addicted to alcohol. Her use of alcohol had not gone beyond the realms of sociological or psychological use. Therefore, when they put her into detox, she had absolutely no withdrawal symptoms of shakes, hallucinations, sweats, nightmares, emotional outbursts, or seizures.

After five or six days of the hospital staff checking only to see if she had the shakes due to withdrawal, Karen was beginning to wonder why the hell she even bothered to check herself in for alcohol treatment. The doctors finally said, "We don't see any symptoms of alcohol dependence. You don't exhibit any withdrawal symptoms so we are going to discharge you."

Karen left the hospital thinking what a waste it all was and went back to her drinking while still taking the Effexor. Effexor can cause effects that may impair your thinking or reactions. Alcohol does the same thing. Mixing the two can more than double the effects of the two drugs.

It didn't take long for Karen to acquire two DUI arrests within a two month period of time. She was sent to me by the courts and after an intake and assessment, it was discovered that Karen's drinking problem was the result of her using alcohol to deal with her unhappiness due to marital problems. She was self-medicating with alcohol to escape from the reality of her failing marriage and all of her past failed attempts to control the situation. As long as she was drinking, she didn't care about her failing marriage until she sobered up.

Karen was not biochemically addicted, yet. But she was relying on alcohol for her emotional and negative thinking, as well as feeling better physically when she felt happier. Left to these behaviors, she would most certainly have become physically addicted. Karen was taught reality therapy and choice theory. The first step towards her treatment was maintaining abstinence while also discovering what she had been doing that was harming her marriage rather than helping it. She began to self-evaluate and look at her own behavior rather than the behavior of others who she had been quick to judge as the cause of her unhappiness. Discovering different ways to behave brought about improvement in her marriage. Self-assessment as well as focusing on those things she felt she wanted in life but didn't have were keys to maintaining her sobriety and bringing her happiness. Once Karen began to acquire happiness and get her needs met, she no longer had the need to self-medicate with alcohol or Effexor.

Why Do We Do <u>Anything</u> That We Do?

All we do from birth until death is behave. And all behavior is chosen. All chosen behaviors are our best attempt, at the time, to make an unpleasant situation pleasant. Another way of saying it is: All behavior serves the purpose of attaining happiness.

If you are a true addict/alcoholic, you will probability want to argue the above statement that all of our behaviors are chosen. In fact, even if you aren't an alcoholic or an addict, you might want to argue the point that we choose all of our behavior. You would probably tell me that if other people didn't say or do some of the things they say or do, that you would not behave in certain ways. With perhaps the exception of anger, all of our emotions are learned. Newborn infants often come into this world not very happy. But even as we mature, anger is an emotion, along with all other emotions, that we can choose to exhibit or not.

You cannot have an emotion without a thought preceding it. With no thoughts, all you would have would be neutral or non-emotional. To experience either happiness or anger, a happy or angry thought has to be present in order to lead to the angry or happy emotion. If you experience anxiety, it's because of what you are thinking. If you suffer from depression, it's because of what you are thinking. If you suffer from Post Traumatic Stress Disorder, it's because of the things you are thinking about. If you suffer from Obsessive Compulsive Disorder, it's because of what you don't want to think about, so you stay busy thinking and doing other things to avoid the thoughts you don't want. If you suffer from any phobia, it's because of what you are thinking.

Here's a little experiment for you to do that I hope will make it easier to understand that you are choosing your emotions: Think of someone, either in the present or the past, whom you do not like. Close your eyes and visualize them in your mind's eye. What are they wearing? What is the expression on their face? What is their body language? After visualizing them for perhaps only 20 or 30 seconds, what do you feel? Are you happy or angry? Most likely, you are angry. Where in your body do you feel your anger or negative emotions when they occur? OK. Have you done the exercise and identified the emotion and where you feel the emotion?

Now I would like you to think of someone who is not physically with you, who exists either in the present or the past whom you really like a lot. Close your eyes and visualize them in your mind's eye. What are they wearing? What is the expression on their face? What is their body language? After 20 or 30 seconds, what do you feel? Most likely, you feel happiness and/or comfort. And where in your body do you feel these positive emotions or happiness when they occur?

Now I would like to point out something to you. The person whom you were thinking about when angry emotions and tense physical reactions in your body occurred is not here. The person whom you were thinking about when you felt happy and comfortable is not here either. So if neither of them is here, how could those people make you feel those two opposite emotions? Your emotions, either negative or positive, came directly from within you, at the top of your limbic system to be exact, based upon whatever thoughts you were having at the time.

What is the most common cause of unhappiness? Someone in your life, someone important to you, and it may even be you, yourself, is behaving in a way that you disapprove of. We could say that unhappiness is the result of unsatisfying relationships with those who are important to us. When you find yourself in this type of situation, the most common thing you do is something that you agreed that you can't do in the last chapter . . . try to control them. Then you put the seven deadly habits into play and all you get is frustration, anger, and a sense of helplessness and hopelessness.

Someone in Al-Anon recently told me, "Don't try to teach a pig to sing. You will only frustrate yourself and piss off the pig" This exemplifies precisely how the seven deadly sins work in our actions and reactions with other people, especially those closest to us.

In the use of Choice Theory, Dr. Glasser (1998) has identified five basic needs that are the motivators of all of our behavior. We are behaving in ways to satisfy these genetic needs. One of the needs is physiological and the other four needs are psychological. We are all hard-wired to have these needs making them genetic in nature. They are:

- Survival
- Love & Belonging
- Power
- Freedom
- Fun

Most of our genes are controlled naturally, or by Mother Nature if you prefer. The shape of our body, our eye color, the formation of our limbs, the color of our hair, and even our personality of fast, slow, or easy going or all taken care of naturally. But the five genetic needs listed above must be learned. They are genetic in that all human beings happen to have these needs regardless of nationality or culture. Those who don't get their genetic needs met will struggle and strive to get them met. If repeated attempts have failed some individuals have a tendency to detach from others . . . to become somewhat "loners." Dr. Glasser refers to this detachment as "disconnectedness." It is this disconnectedness that will be the underlying core issue or cause of their unhappiness. They find creative ways to get their genetic needs met in other ways. Alcohol and drugs are a common method to compensate for unmet needs.

Unlike Abe Maslow's ascending hierarchy of needs, there is no hierarchy of these basic, genetic needs. Wubboldidng (1999) makes the case that if humans always satisfied their need for survival as a primary need and ahead of the other needs, there would be no one committing suicide. Suicide is the ultimate form of disconnectedness and a common reason for this behavior is due to desperate feelings of loneliness - the need for love and belonging.

Survival (the physiological need)

Besides the basic will to survive in the worst of circumstances, we have other needs such as food, shelter, clothing, reproduction, transportation, and an income to help provide us with these needs. We have to LEARN a career or job that will afford us these needs. Nature doesn't necessarily teach us how to do that. However, if we don't have the survival needs met, we will behave in any number of ways in attempts to get them met. Many people have the capability of becoming comfortable in uncomfortable situations. They have learned to tolerate their misery or unhappiness. Their genetic need of survival can be very low and therefore they may not be motivated to strive above and beyond their perceived capabilities to improve their survival needs.

I'm reminded of the story, the teller of which I can not recall, of a young man who was walking down the street when he began to hear a sorrowful moaning and groaning sound. He began to look around to see where the source of this sound was coming from. On the other side of the street was an elderly man sitting on the steps of his front porch reading a newspaper. Lying next to the old guy was a hound dog. The young man approached the older man and said:

"Is that your dog moaning and groaning?"

The old man replied, "Yup."

The younger man asked, "Is there something wrong with him?"

The older man said, "He's layin' on a nail."

"Then why doesn't he get up and move?" asked the younger man.

The old man replied, "Cause he ain't hurtin' bad enough yet."

How many times have you found yourself lying on a nail, moaning and groaning, but not hurting badly enough to do anything about it?

Others may have ample income to afford their needs of survival so they may not be so driven to strive for any improvement in these needs. It appears that those who struggle the most for their survival in our American culture are those that have not acquired the proper tools to get this need met. They have tried several different ways to meet this need but for any number of reasons, they simply accept what they have or even quit trying. Still others may attempt the easy way to acquiring their survival needs by stealing, raping, murdering, cheating, blackmailing, robbing, etc. They will also have high power needs as well.

Some of the things that keeps people from getting their survival needs met are a lack of education and not willing to acquire it; isolating or detaching from others, and seeing the need for help from others as a weakness; choosing to depress rather than do what they know they must do to improve their situation; relying on drugs or alcohol to fool their mind into believing these needs are being met.

Of all the survival needs sex, or reproduction, is the only one that is not learned in order to acquire it. Mother Nature has a way of taking care of that and even a virus will struggle to reproduce before it dies. Skillful and satisfying sex, on the other hand, is learned. However, there is another form of sex that is not genetic and it falls under a different genetic category of Power, which you will see later.

As long as the alcoholic/addict continues to get his drug on a regular basis, he feels he has all the survival he needs. He may even feel that it is because of his drug of choice that he is able to meet his survival needs. He relies on them psychologically to convince him that he is bigger and better than he really is so that he can impress others and "make things happen." This, however, is only a short-term situation. Eventually the continued use will take its toll physically, mentally, spiritually, and he will lose all he has. A common thought of alcoholics/addicts is, "Everything I used to touch used to turn to gold. Now it all turns to shit. What the hell happened?" From this point on, he will only strive to maintain the least of his survival needs with the exception of the strong need to survive via the continued use of his drug of choice.

The addiction to a drug or alcohol also causes the need for food to diminish. Depending upon the intensity of the addiction, sex is even forgone for sake of the drug and/or the inability to perform the act itself. The interest is lost. Anyone who drinks/uses long enough and hard enough will eventually diminish their survival needs. Many even resort to suicide.

Love & Belonging

The need for love and the need to belong and relate to others is one of the strongest genetic needs we have. I contend that how well we get these needs met will have a direct effect upon how well we receive all the other needs.

There are two kinds of love. (Glasser 2003) Family love (genetic) is that love which we naturally have for our parents and siblings and their love for us. It may also be why we humans are so social in nature. We have a need to belong or identify with different groups and to socialize. Romantic love, however, is something that is learned. We love others as a direct result of our own past experience of receiving love from others. If you never received much love, you will not have much love to give or show. If you have very few friends, you have not learned how to love very well. One can not readily give what one has never received. All they would be giving is what they think it "might be like" if they had it to give.

Finding someone to love is the easy part. Many a person will look at a stranger or a photo of someone and declare their love for that person without even knowing them. They are drawn to them for physical traits, station in life, financial and/or material assets, or their celebrity status. They may even remind them of someone from their past whom Harville Hendrix (1990) refers to as "The Imago." Finding love is easy. The difficult part of love is finding someone who is willing to love us in return.

Those who have a history of failed relationships that tend to end with subsequent depression, anger, despair, and misery will eventually give up using their past skills to achieve the need for love and belonging. They will tend to detach from others, convince themselves they don't need another person in their life, and find other ways of meeting this need.

The majority of so-called mental illness diagnoses given to people are no more than people who have no satisfying relationships with the important people in their lives. Their behavior, which is seen as strange or odd, is considered to be due to some form of chemical imbalance or insanity when actually, it is only that person's best attempt at the time to bring them happiness.

Power

We all have the need for power only in different amounts. Power is the result of one who has or receives the respect and appreciation from others. And the people who give this respect and appreciation don't mind doing so because they see him as one who is deserving of their respect and appreciation. But there are those who don't have the respect they feel they should have or are getting and they choose to behave in ways to force others to respect them through fear or intimidation and threats.

The power we need in our lives is for a sense of achievement and worthiness. Some people have strong power needs as seen in their competitiveness. There is the power to do, the power to acquire, and the power over others. But the power we need for happiness is the power to control ourselves to acquire a sense of importance, pride, and accomplishment without imposing or taking these same powers away from others: The power of healthy respect.

Sadam Hussein intimidated his country populace by fear of death, beatings, and imprisonment in order to give him the power he wanted. It was effective as long as he was able to intimidate them. This means he had to continually intimidate and enforce his power over others in order to maintain it. Once he was captured and removed, the respect that he got from power ended from a great deal of many people. But then, another group of people moved in, Al-Qaida, and brought more intimidation than Hussein was utilizing in an attempt to gain power over the people.

We humans have a tendency to fight about anything and everything. Nothing is more completely inane than war or a bar fight. The outcome, one way or the other, proves nothing and both individuals get hurt or worse, killed. No one wins in a fight. They both walk away thinking each of them is right and the other person is wrong.

Every war that has ever existed was due to the use of power as a result of the seven deadly habits. "If you don't do what we want you to do, we're gonna kill you. We aren't murderers. We just know what's better for you than you do. We're going to shove Democracy down your throat whether you want it or not because we think it is better than what you currently have." The minute we begin to think that we know what is right for other people other than ourselves is when we begin to have conflict.

Every marriage that has ever ended in divorce did so because of the use of Power and the seven deadly habits.

Each felt they knew what was better for the other person and each wanted the other to stop doing something that they disapproved of.

Some individuals use material possessions, and sex to give them a sense of self-worth and they expect to receive admiration, envy, and respect for what they own, measured in dollars and cents instead of the worth of the individual as a person. Some men may acquire a sense of masculinity, self-worth, and power based upon the number of women they bed. Still others may rape women and rape is no less than a behavior of power over them.

It has been my experience that even though we may be upset or in conflict with someone else of importance to our lives, that this, alone, is not enough to cause someone to drink or use drugs to the point of addiction. While certainly conflict with others is often used as an excuse to drink, or to calm down after an angry encounter, the real problem appears to be rooted in one's own low self-worth and intense feelings of shame and guilt. These are perceptions that are not easy to outrun because they are in our own head. This is why many alcoholics and addicts don't like to be alone (at first) because they don't like living in their own head. When we are alone, the only person we are in touch with is our self. And if you don't like yourself, you don't like to be alone with yourself. It's so much easier to get outside your head when in the presence of others because then you don't have to listen to your own thoughts and think about your own disowned parts of yourself that you don't like. Later on, however, during the later stages of addiction, the addict/alcoholic becomes a loner because s/he doesn't want you to know how often or how much s/he drinks/uses. So they drink/use where you can't see them. They may also have detached from all of their long time drinking buddies (the non-problem drinking friends left a long time ago) and isolate until they die or get help.

Freedom

Freedom is also a basic need. If you think it's not important, experience what it's like to be locked up in a small jail cell. Go to a country that has much less freedom than America. The old saying, "you don't know what you've got until you lose it" is never more true when it comes to the loss of freedom.

Freedom is the ability to come and go as you please as long as it does not impinge upon the rights of others. Freedom allows you to make your own choices . . . to have the autonomy to do what you feel is right for you but not to impose it on others. Freedom allows you to travel to any place you desire. Freedom is doing what you want to do as long as it does not break any laws or harms others. Freedom means that you have choices with nothing to stop you.

Fun

The genetic reward for fun is learning. (Glasser, 1998) Looking back on your formal education, it would be fairly safe to say that your favorite classes and favorite teachers were those who made the class fun. We tend to learn and retain knowledge of those things that were taught by a teacher who knew how to make the subjects fun.

Fun and recreation are an important part of our lives that creates happiness in what can otherwise be considered a busy world with no time except to survive and be powerful. Fun keeps us in touch with the world and ourselves in a way that keeps us from taking ourselves and our world too seriously. Fun is an important part of breaking up the monotony of routine behaviors. Fun is enjoying your job or career. It serves to recharge us, to motivate us and give more energy to do the things we need to do to maintain our happiness and interaction with others. Learning to have fun is also a way of learning to be able to laugh at ourselves and our mistakes.

The above five basic needs are those things that motivate all humans and are the ultimate reason why we behave the way we do . . . in an attempt to get these needs met. It bears repeating: All behavior is our best attempt at the time to bring the result of happiness . . . by satisfying one or more of the five genetic needs.

If you are involved with an alcoholic or an addict, you have been trying to force your power over them by trying to get them to quit. And just like all of the examples cited above, the result of utilizing power over others will always have disastrous results. You then begin to feel "powerless." If you are a strong power driven person, this sense of powerlessness leads to you choosing anger or depression. Your anger will either be expressed outwardly or you will want to keep your anger in check so as not to harm yourself or anyone else. Anger turned inwardly manifests itself by choosing to depress and keep your anger in control.

When we see a discrepancy between the real world and our Quality Word images and values, we get a sense of frustration or, if you will, unhappiness. We then begin to behave in ways to attempt to make the real world images match the images and values in our Quality World. We do this by attempting to satisfy one or more of the genetic needs. We then resort to our Tool Kit and begin utilizing tools that we have used in the past that have resolved other, if not similar, image discrepancies.

The most common ways people express their unhappiness is with physical pain. The second most common way people express their unhappiness is through creative behaviors that serve a purpose to meet one or more of their basic needs. People do things that work for them or they wouldn't do them. The problem is that you can't see what purpose these behaviors serve so they are often called mental illnesses. The purpose of these behaviors will always fall within one or more of their unmet basic needs. The behavior people choose is meant to close the gap between what they want and what they don't have.

Your Tool Kit

Can you hammer a nail with a rock? Can you hammer a nail with a pair of pliers? Can you hammer a nail with a shoe, or the butt end of a screwdriver? Of course you can. A hammer is obviously the best tool to use to hammer a nail. But if you don't have a hammer, you might be inclined to use any of the other tools I mentioned to get the job done.

The human mind can be very creative when it comes to meeting our unmet genetic needs. Over the years, we have created a sort of tool chest. This tool chest consists of all the tools we have picked up and used to solve past difficulties in our lives. Any time we are faced with a situation that causes a general feeling of unhappiness, we reach into our tool chest in an effort to fix whatever it is that is making us unhappy.

When faced with the conflict of images (the real world vs. our quality world), and the frustration that is felt, we reach in our tool kit and use it to fix the unmatched images. In our toolkit are such things as a rock, pliers, screwdriver, shoe, hammer, alcohol, and drugs of various kinds. If one tool doesn't work, we reach for another. If that doesn't work, we keep reaching for all the tools that we have in our kit. When all of the tools we possess have been tried and failed, we get creative and start making our own tools to deal with the frustration. The tools they create can be behaviors that have been labeled as depression, anxiety, obsessive compulsive behavior, other personality disorders, Attentive Deficit Disorder (ADD,) Attention Deficit Hyperactivity Disorder (ADHD,) schizophrenia, Bi-Polar, etc.

People do what works. In other words, their behavior serves a purpose or else they wouldn't do it. It may not be the best results they would like, but it does the job for the time being, until they can come up with a better tool. The problem is that we don't always see how the behavior of others is working for them. And since most people can't see how it is working, they have a tendency to think the person is "crazy" or "mentally ill and needs medication." The tools they devise to create their happiness may not be the best tools for the job, but they work to some satisfying degree or they wouldn't do them.

If you looked outside your window and you saw someone dancing as they walked down the street and you heard no music, would you say to yourself or to someone else, 'that guy's crazy.' If you did, you would not be taking into consideration why he may be dancing. He may be wearing earphones on his iPod and dancing to the music that you can't hear. He may be happy that he just got promoted or a raise at work. He may have just fallen in love. He may have just won the lottery. He may be dancing to the music in his head because he feels so happy at the moment. But we are so quick to pass judgment and diagnose them as mentally ill, see him as a threat to our own happiness and security, think he needs to be on medication, and want to see him institutionalized.

If you are a golfer, all anyone would have to do, whether you are on the golf course or not, is yell "FORE!" and you'd duck and cover instantly out of conditioning. People who have been diagnosed with Post Traumatic Stress Disorder (PTSD) have been conditioned to hear people yelling "FORE" all the time and at the most inopportune moments. Are they mentally ill? No. They are doing what works for them based upon the conditioning they have to survive as perceived in a threatening world. Their real world and quality world images do not match and their behavior is an attempt to satisfy their genetic need to survive. Their thoughts are ever-present to stay ready in order to keep from having to get ready in order to ward off any possible attack. They are anxiety ridden. As stated earlier, one can not have anxiety unless one is thinking of things that affect their emotions of anxiety and cause their physiology to react as well.

If you feel you have not lived the life you should have lived or if you see yourself as unloved, unlovable, inadequate, incapable, a screw-up, and possess a lot of shame and guilt, you will reach in your tool kit in order to make any of these thoughts and corresponding physiological reactions go away. Somewhere in your past, you learned very early that alcohol or drugs are wonderful for making these unwanted thoughts and corresponding emotions and physical reactions go away. In fact, nothing works faster at eradicating these unwanted thoughts, emotions, and reactions. This tool works so well that you keep it at the top of all of your tools in your tool kit. However, it has limitations. It only works for as long as it is in your body and brain. When you sober up, all of these unwanted feelings and thoughts and reactions return . . . worse than the last time you had them. This is why you have to keep using that tool in order for it to be effective.

If you perceive yourself as a victim or as the cause of anyone or everyone else's dissatisfaction, you will also find this tool (alcohol/drugs) to work effectively for making you feel better as long as you are using it.

When we see others who have been diagnosed as bipolar, obsessive compulsive, schizophrenic, personality disordered, or any number of other possible DSM IV diagnoses for mental illness, what we are really seeing are people who are unhappy. . . people who are having difficulty with their relationships . . . people who are in conflict with others who are important to them who are behaving in ways that are unacceptable to them.

A man was driving along a highway when he suddenly had a tire blow out. He pulled over to the side of the road that just happened to be the front acreage of a mental hospital. The weeds along the side of the road were very tall and they separated him from a wooden fence that went around the perimeter of the hospital. He got out of his car, took out the jack and spare tire and began to jack the car up in order to change the tire. It was at this time that one of the mental hospital patients walked down to the front of the highway and rested his head on his palms that were supported by his elbows on the top of the fence. He merely watched with interest as the motorist began to loosen and remove the lug nuts from the flat tire and place them in the wheel cover so that he wouldn't lose them.

It wasn't long that by the time he took off the 5th lug nut that his back began to ache. He stood up to stretch his aching back muscles and as he did, his heel caught the rim of the wheel cover containing the lug nuts and sent them flying in all directions in the tall weeds and grass. No matter how hard he tired, he couldn't locate them.

"That's just great," he uttered. "What the hell am I going to do now?"

The mental patient replied, "Why don't you take one lug nut off of the other three tires and use them to put on the spare until you can get into town and replace them?"

The motorist was amazed. "That's a hell of an idea. I never would have thought of that. What's a guy like you doing in a place like this hospital?"

The patient responded, "I'm here 'cause I'm crazy, not because I'm stupid."

Depression

This is a good spot to talk about depression. Alcoholics consume a liquid that is a depressant drug. If alcohol were invented today, you would need a prescription to buy it tomorrow. The effects of alcohol are often more severe than many other prescription drugs that are given out by doctors on a regular basis. If you drink alcohol, it will start out by lowering your inhibitions, begin to excite one's emotions, and you will sense some euphoria. This is why most people drink it in the first place. But too much alcohol or when the effects of alcohol begin to wear off, the depressant aspect of the drug begins.

However, and this is important, you don't have to be an alcoholic to experience depression. With the exception of the drug's depressant tendencies, all other forms of depression are chosen emotions.

Are you that person that is still living and loving that alcoholic or addict of yours? How happy have you been choosing to be the last few months or several years of your life? You always have a choice in how you react to the information that is being put into your mind by your perception of what is happening. Many people think that the opposite of love is hate. However, if it were hate, you would still have an emotional attachment due to your perception of the loss of love. The opposite of love in not hate, it's "indifference." Indifference is a neutral emotion and the result of not having an emotional tie to anyone or thing. Love, hate, indifference, and any other emotion you may think of are emotions and all emotions are chosen.

Why Would I Choose to be Depressed?

Dr. Glasser (1998) best explains it. He explains that depression serves three purposes:

Choosing to depress is a way of asking for help, without actually coming out and asking for help. Have you ever seen a depressed person? Of course you have. You don't even have to know them personally. You can distinguish a depressed person by their facial expression, body language, and their tone and manner of speech. If a friend of yours appeared before you and you noticed the signs and symptoms of depression, you would most likely say, "What's happening? Are you OK?" Your friend just got help without having to ask you for it.

Choosing to depress also serves the purpose of downgrading your anger or, keeping it in check. If it weren't for depression, we would have a lot more murder, assault, property damage, etc. in the world. One of the dangers, of which there are many, of putting someone on an antidepressant, is the possible release of their anger. Just look at Andrea Yates who drowned her five children or the two boys from Columbine High School who shot students and teachers. Antidepressants were involved in both cases and the list goes on and on.

The third reason why many people choose to depress, and this is quite common, is because there is something or someone going on in your life that is causing you to choose unhappiness and you know specifically what you have to do about the situation to make it better. . . but you don't want to. You may also be reluctant to want to accept a situation realistically. You would rather live with the unhappiness than make necessary changes or to accept the reality of a situation to improve your happiness and wellbeing. Alcoholics do this all the time. You do it all the time too if you live with or are in love with an alcoholic or an addict. Another example would be when a person has lost a dear friend, spouse, or family member. They may mourn for years because they are reluctant to "let go" of the pain of their loss. It's almost as if they feel that by letting go, they will forget them or that by letting go, it will mean that they didn't really love them . . . neither of which is necessarily true.

The alcoholic or addict knows they have to quit but they are not willing to give it up for fear of withdrawals, fear of what will happen if they quit, fear of how to cope with life and stress without their drug. The person who lives with or loves the alcohol/addict sees their only solution as leaving the person they love and they don't want to do that due to fear of supporting themselves and/or children, no where to go due to no family or friends, or lack of finances.

Marilyn was the mother of a 33 year old son, James, who had two sons as well. James was divorced and was the custodial parent of two boys. Both James and his ex wife had been involved in severe methamphetamine and alcohol dependence. James was still using and drinking and his mother, Marilyn, was at her wits end. She had done all of the seven deadly habits to get James to quit and to be a better father to his boys. She feared what would happen to her grandsons with James' continued use.

One day, Marilyn mentioned in an email to me that she was having some problems with her son because of his methamphetamine and alcohol use. Since Marilyn was a friend of mine as well as living some 1500 miles away, I could not ethically offer her any therapy. However, I did give her a suggestion and that was to find an Al-Anon meeting after having explained to her what it is and what it does.

Several weeks went by and I discovered that Marilyn had still not gone to an Al-Anon meeting and was still feeling miserable, depressed, and powerless over her son's drug and alcohol use. I went online and found an Al-Anon meeting very close to Marilyn's home and sent her the address and times the meetings were being held. Marilyn did go and came back with much exuberance about her experience with the meeting. I knew it would have a positive effect on her but I didn't expect it to be so much so quickly, and after only one meeting. She began going on a regular basis and also, at my suggestion, purchased a copy of Dr. Glasser's Choice Theory.

Al-Anon and Choice Theory brought back the happiness Marilyn had lost due to feeling powerless and fearful of James' and her grandsons' future. As soon as she stopped utilizing the seven deadly habits to get James to stop his substance use, he began the process of stopping because no one was hounding him or nagging him to quit. James began to feel better and found that with no one nagging or complaining, he was less depressed and felt more capable to address his use of drugs and alcohol. By choosing to stop employing the seven deadly habits, Marilyn was able to cease her choice of depressing to deal with her powerlessness in getting James to quit. James decided that he no longer needed to depress because he didn't want to have to be angry with his mother.

Marilyn's story is an excellent example of how Choice Theory works in dealing with our relationships with others. When one person stops doing something that is harmful to the relationship, the other person will almost always stop behaving in ways to counteract the behavior that harms the relationship even more.

Our Quality World

Each of us has what Dr. Glasser, (1998) calls our Quality World. Inside our quality world are images . . . pictures in our mind of all of those things that bring us happiness. The images in our quality world are our wants and our values. We are the only ones who put these images in our quality world and, conversely, we are the only ones who can take any images out of it.

Our quality world contains such things as images of our self, our family, our parents, our spouse, our best friend, our ideal career or job, our favorite vacation whether you have even been there or not, our values, etc. Each of us possesses similar images with others as well as totally different images in our quality world. Our quality world is always changing. Remember the last time you got dumped in a relationship? Someone had taken you out of their quality world. Try as you may have, they didn't put you back in. Eventually, you had to accept the reality of the situation and then take them out of your quality world and you found someone else to replace the image. It's important to understand that only until you took them out of your quality world did you begin to feel better and get over your depression of the loss of the relationship.

The real world is that world which presents itself to us in ways that may be different than what we perceive in our quality world. Whenever we have a picture of the real world that does not meet our quality world image, we tend to feel a little glitch . . . an uncomfortable feeling or "frustration" and we know something is not right. All of the clients I have in my practice have this "frustration." There is a difference between what they want and what they have.

When we compare what we have as to what we want, the difference will cause a physical reaction based upon the emotion we choose to deal with the difference we see. Remember my client who didn't see his drinking as a problem? He wasn't feeling any frustration. He feels he is just fine and it's everyone else who is frustrated. He's right about one thing: Everyone in his life IS frustrated because of his drinking. So he simply chooses not to feel upset and let everyone else in his life do all of the frustrating.

Right now, I feel quite confident that someone just woke up and said, "Hey, wait a minute, Rice. Did you just say 'the emotion we *choose?*' Are you telling me that we choose our emotions?" (I've been saying it repeatedly throughout this book).

The answer to your question is yes. We don't choose it directly but rather indirectly based upon what it is that we are thinking or what we are doing at the time. Our emotions are only a part of our total behavior and since all of our behavior is chosen, we are also choosing our emotions. Ooops! I just woke up someone else. Even though I have said it several times earlier, you may have just let it glide by. But now you want to challenge me about the statement about us choosing our behavior.

When the phone rings, do you have to answer it? When the traffic light turns red, do you have to stop? Can someone else really piss you off? You may want to argue the point and say, "yes, they do." Alcoholics love to argue. It gives them a sense of power in a world that appears powerless to them. All that the phone and traffic light does is give you information. The information is: Someone is calling you, or traffic is now going to move from the other direction. Information does not make you behave. You choose whether or not you want to answer the phone or stop at the light, knowing what the result may be if you don't.

No one can piss you off unless you choose to be pissed off. You can just as easily choose not to be pissed off as you can to choose to do otherwise. Someone said or did something which gave you information and that information did not make you get pissed off. You have the ability to receive information and choose how you want to react to it. You could have reacted neutrally and let it not affect you one way or the other. You could have reacted by perceiving the situation as being humorous rather than insulting, or defiant, or any other negative perception.

The alcoholic or the addict will always have their drug of choice in their quality world. They are the only ones who can take this pleasurable picture out of their quality world. This is why you and others have failed in all of your past attempts to get them to quit. It is also why the addict/alcoholic fails to get sober. He doesn't want to take the drug or alcohol out of his quality world. Taking something out of your quality world usually means having to put something else in its place. He doesn't know what to replace his alcohol or drug use with, yet.

When you lose a girlfriend or boyfriend, you usually replace him or her with someone else. The other alternative is to detach from others and not put anyone in there at all. But the addict or the alcoholic must replace it with something else besides another drug or brand of alcohol. Some people replace their image of their drug with a twelve step program. Others attach to their faith and religion. Still others may find something else to become addicted to such as coffee, tea, food, sports, work, sex, or spending just to name a few. I don't know anyone who had only one addiction.

To recap the Quality World, it is our personal container of all of the things that we feel that bring us happiness. . . and those things that are "right" for us. We use it to compare the things that make us happy to the things that are occurring outside of ourselves in the real world. If what is perceived in the real world matches our image in our quality world, we are happy. If the two images don't match, we start to feel frustrated. Then we choose actions that we believe will make the two images match, or at least match a little closer than they currently do.

If what we do is effective, we find happiness or a decrease in our frustration. If what we do does not work, we only feel more frustration and perhaps more intense than what we first felt. We keep trying to resolve our frustration with different tools that we have used over the years. If we have finally utilized all of our tools and still nothing has worked, we start making our own new tools hoping that one or more of them will ease our frustration. The mind can be very creative when trying to find new tools.

Some of the ways that people devise new tools to deal with their frustration is in the form of what others call Mental Illness. They are behaving in ways that may appear odd or outright "crazy" to others so they label the person as "mentally ill." They are often sent to mental health agencies where they don't receive mental health; they receive a mental illness diagnosis and are put on medication. There will be no pathology for their diagnosis other than someone who diagnosed them as mentally ill. There will be no lab tests or any radiology, or biochemical tests to prove the existence of mental illness other than someone said so. Even the DSM IV, the book written by psychiatrists and used by all mental health delivery personnel, sates that no laboratory findings exist that are capable of diagnosing any of the conditions that are called mental illness.

What the person suffers from is not mental illness. S/he is suffering from an unsatisfying relationship and doing the best s/he can at the moment to find happiness and feel better. What you or someone else reading this book did was reach for a bottle or a drug to cause your unhappiness to go away. You are not mentally ill. Your behavior, however, depending upon what you are drinking or using will often mimic behaviors that appear to be out of the realm of "normal" behavior, further causing others to label you as mentally ill or crazy. For this type of diagnosis, you don't need psychiatric drugs. You just need to get clean and sober.

Alcoholics Anonymous

Here's the part in the book that many readers will start to shut down and close off their thinking. A large block will come up and keep them from any positive information that may just save their life. What is it about A.A. that turns so many people off?

The answer to the question is: Ignorance. Say the letters "AA" to some people and they pull up any number of negative images. I used to be just like that, myself, so I can relate. To some people, A.A. conjures up images of "Skid Row Bums." Do you know what percentage of alcoholics fit that category? Approximately 3%. The majority of alcoholics and addicts look just like you and me. They are doctors, lawyers, teachers, clergy, police officers, construction workers, nurses, office workers, business men and women, retailers, etc. You name the career or profession and someone who does that is a member of A.A.

Here's another often heard remark: All they do is sit around and feel sorry for themselves and tell old war stories. For those of you who perceive that their stories are feeling sorry for themselves, your information filter has kept you from seeing what is actually going on in the telling of those stories. The stories you hear at an A.A. meeting are not for the person telling the story so much as it is for showing others what drinking can lead to, the stupid things it makes you do, and may even be very similar experience to another person who just started to come into A.A. and saw himself and his behavior due to the other person's stories.

A.A. has been around since 1935. It is solely supported by its members. They don't advertise. They don't ask for donations from the public. They believe in anonymity to protect your privacy. They care about you when no one else does. They understand you when you feel no one else does. They have gone through, and more, what you have even though you may not believe it.

Several programs addressing alcoholism and addiction have come and gone but Alcoholics Anonymous (A.A.), Narcotics Anonymous (N.A.), and Cocaine Anonymous (C.A.) are still here. A.A. has stood the test of time for over 73 years. No other program can make that claim. They must be doing something right to endure this long.

A.A. contains 12 steps, or tasks, to complete to bring sobriety and sanity back to the life of the addict and alcoholic. Many people can stop drinking or using drugs but to not do the 12 steps only makes them what we call in recovery, "Dry Drunks." A dry drunk is someone who continues to behave the way he always has even though he is not currently drinking or using. They failed to work the 12 step program and acquire recovery skills. All they did was quit drinking.

Dave tells the story of his brother-in-law, Jerry, an ex hard core drinker. Dave reported that his brother-in-law use to drink anywhere from 3 quarts to 6 quarts of beer a day when he came home from work. Jerry had wrecked four cars in 6 years when drunk. He lost his job as a teacher due to the number of DUI charges he acquired. His alcohol use affected is wife by her becoming a complete control freak . . . trying to control everything and anything in her life because she couldn't control his drinking. Finally, after years of putting up with his drunken behavior and the harm it was causing the family, she threatened to leave him if he didn't quit.

Jerry quit, according to Dave, but he didn't go to A.A. He didn't want to go because he was afraid of being recognized and people would find out that he was an alcoholic. Jerry was still thinking like a drunk. Everyone already knew that Jerry was the town drunk. They had known it for years.

Dave would describe Jerry as a know-it-all similar to Cliff Claven from the TV show Cheers. He further would describe Jerry as a pompous SOB similar to Major Charles Emerson Winchester from the TV show M.A.S.H. And he said, "My best description of Jerry would be, 'Asshole.'"

Dave further reported that once Dave had owned a tan colored Cadillac. He then purchased a Buick of the same color several years later. His brother-in-law, Jerry, saw the new Buick and seeing the same color said, "Boy you sure do like your Cadillacs." Dave responded, "Yeah, but THIS Cadillac is a Buick." Jerry quickly responded, "I know that." Then Jerry went on to talk about the time that he, Dave, Dave's sister and their parents drove to the Grand Canyon and how well that old Cadillac held up driving all around the area. Dave said, "I've lived in Arizona for over 24 years and I have never been to the Grand Canyon in my life." Then he said, "My brother-in-law was an asshole when he drank. He doesn't drink anymore but he's still an asshole."

There is a lot more to recovery than simply stopping the use of drugs or alcohol. There are several sociological and personal behaviors that need to be developed. There is the need to rid one's self of all of the shame and guilt they have been carrying around for years. There are boundaries that need to be learned. There are methods that need to be developed to learn how to have fun without the use of drugs or alcohol. There are several emotions that need to be learned to identify and how to deal with them in a healthy manner rather than drugs or alcohol. There are relationship issues that need to be learned. These things are learned via the 12 steps of A.A.

The program, after you get sober, is to "work" the 12 steps. Take them one at a time and not rush through them. This is the time that you will want to find a sponsor . . .another member of A.A. who has adequate abstinence and can explain and walk you through the steps. Your sponsor is also someone whom you can call when you feel like drinking, using, or just going crazy. Your sponsor is your personal friend and teacher to get you through the rough spots.

A.A. is an excellent place to meet new sober friends whom you can relate to and who can relate to you. If you go to a meeting and you do not feel comfortable there, find another meeting somewhere else. Look in the yellow pages under alcohol and you will usually find the central A.A. phone number who can tell you where the meetings are in your area. They will even send you an A.A. meeting lists of all of the meetings and the times, days, and locations of where they meet.

Choice Theory is so very compatible with A.A. They both deal with knowing what you can control and what you can't. They both place a lot of emphasis on the need for meaningful relationships.

A word of warning about relationships in A.A.: Keep your relationships non-obligatory and non-sexual with the opposite gender. Too often, people get romantically involved in A.A. thinking that they can support and help one another in their recovery. This is referred to as "Thirteen Steppin.'" The problem with his way of thinking is that you have the blind leading the blind. In principal, it may sound good to be helping one another but the help we need in recovery must come from someone who has recovered and not freshly learned. Being responsible for your own recovery is difficult enough without getting involved in someone else's.

Thirteen Steppers are only attempting to satisfy their basic need of love and to deal with their current loneliness. Relationships are great and they are greatly needed to maintain happiness, but right now, if you are just now going through abstinence of less than a year or two, I highly recommend that you not get involved in a sexual relationship until you have more sobriety and more recovery and also have learned about non-obligatory relationships. (More on this in a later chapter)

Can I get sober without A.A. or 12 Step Meetings?

Sobriety is absolutely attainable without A.A. but as I have said several times before, sobriety is the easy part. The hard part is recovery and that you can't always get in other programs or on your own.

A.A. is not the best program for alcohol/drug addiction. Does that surprise you that I say that? I say it because the best has not been invented yet. To date, A.A. is what works best for most. A.A., along with outpatient or inpatient treatment and counseling, has the strongest makings for overcoming additions than anything else currently available.

If someone were to tell me that they were able to overcome the dependency to drugs or alcohol by standing on their head for fifteen minutes a day, I would say, 'Knock your self out. Do whatever works.'

There are other programs such as the Veterans Hospital, The Salvation Army, Rational Recovery, SMART Recovery, and many churches that have put together programs for addiction. Check your yellow pages for other programs in your area under Alcohol and/or Drug Treatment.

There are several different types of drug and alcohol rehab. Some are inpatient programs, others are outpatient programs. Some are faith based and others are not. Some use methods that have been used in the psychiatric delivery system, and others do not. Some are support groups while still others may incorporate the use of hypnotism, acupuncture, or holistic treatment. To me, alcoholism and drug addiction are not mental illnesses. Nor are they character disorders. They are behaviors that some people have chosen to use to deal with the unhappiness in their life and since these substances are addictive, they have become socially, psychologically, and physically addicted to them.

The reason why so many see it as a mental illness is because of the behaviors they see the addicted people do. They aren't mentally ill. They are only behaving in drug affected ways . . . ways that they would not choose if they were sober. One of the most common errors I see today is therapists, psychologists, and psychiatrists diagnosing methamphetamine clients as schizophrenic based upon their behavior. Methamphetamine does the quickest amount of damage in the least amount of time than any other drug out there. The behaviors it can cause people to do can be so bazaar that one would think they were schizophrenic if they were a lay person. Apparently, many professionals do so as well.

But even in the DSM IV, it is written that clients must meet certain criteria before being diagnosed any of the "mental illnesses" in the book, that the behavior IS NOT the result of drug or alcohol use. Mental Health professionals don't seem to read their own criteria for making diagnoses. More often than not, I have been sent clients who have been placed on thorizine for a diagnosis for schizophrenia even though the therapist or psychiatrist is aware of the client's history of methamphetamine use.

Bill came to me his first day in group. He was introduced to the other group members and given the group's policies. When I asked him if he had any questions, he replied, "I just want to let you know that once in a while, my phone rings and I have to answer it."

I informed Bill that we don't allow the use of phones, pagers, iPods, or any other electronic device while group is in session. He then stated, "But you don't understand. This phone comes out of my rib cage and I have to answer it whether you say I can or not." I looked at Bill and said, let's talk about this. I asked Bill to follow me to the men's room where I had him provide me with a urine sample. He blew the doors off of the drug test card as being positive for methamphetamine. I sent him home and told him not to return until he was capable of supplying a clean urine analysis. He went to a different agency that doesn't test clients for drugs and they sent him to the State's Mental Health agency for schizophrenia.

Unfortunately, I am referred many clients who have been placed on psychiatric medications when they are only unhappy people. They are not mentally ill but the psychiatric delivery system we have stresses co-morbidity (psychiatric issues besides alcohol or drugs). Alcohol and drugs causes behaviors that appear to be psychiatric because they are not normal or customary behaviors. What you are seeing is someone who is behaving based upon drug affected behavior. To diagnoses mental illness when one is under the influence of a drug will always result in an incorrect diagnosis. Diagnoses are made by observation of behavior only with absolutely no regard whatsoever to the existence of any pathology to substantiate the illness. How many of you would take your doctor's word for it that you have cancer and must begin chemotherapy even though no tests were given and no pathology existed to show that you had cancer?

Total Behavior

When it comes to Choice Theory, behavior is seen as having four separate components. (Glasser, 1998) First we think. Secondly, there is an emotion (positive, negative, or neutral). You can not have an emotion without a thought existing before it. Thirdly, there is physiology going on in our body, and fourthly, we have acting. Of these four components, two of them can be directly controlled: Our thoughts and our acting. The other two components we control indirectly. .

The four components are referred to by Dr. Glasser (1998) as, "Total Behavior." He describes behavior as being compared to that of a car. The front wheels are those things that we control with the steering wheel. Since they are controllable, the front wheels would be our thoughts and our behavior. The rear wheels would be our emotions and physiology. Whichever way we turn the front wheels, the rear wheels would have to follow. Therefore the choices we make by controlling the front wheels will have an indirect effect on controlling the rear wheels.

If you are depressing, it's because of what it is that you are thinking. If you are panicking, it's because of what you are thinking. If you are paranoid, it's because of what you are thinking. If you are happy it is because of what you are thinking. If you are obsessing, it's because of what you are thinking. In fact, most of the so-called mental illnesses are the result of unhappy relationships and accompanying unhappy thoughts.

Your emotions and physiology are your indicators that let you know if you have made the correct action. If you turn left and it doesn't feel right or good, or you have a negative physical (gut feeling) reaction to your left turn, then you may want to make another choice in which direction to turn . . . either right or straight ahead.

Just as I was writing this chapter, my phone rang. A woman was calling because her husband was behaving in ways that were frightening her. I asked her if he had threatened to harm her and she replied, "Oh, no, nothing like that. He's just behaving weirdly. I think he's schizophrenic. He has caused me to have fibromyalgia. What should I do?"

She had part of it right: She was suffering physically because of her unhappiness but he didn't cause her to have it. She had simply run out of ways to deal with her husband's behavior and out of all of her frustration came helplessness and aches and pains. Obviously, her husband is behaving in ways unaccustomed to his wife that are meant to satisfy his unmet and frustrating genetic basic needs. He ran out of his regular tools to resolve his own unhappiness and is now creating new tools to deal with it by his "schizophrenic" behavior. Her tools became ineffective and she created aches and pains which she refers to as fibromyalgia. In other words, none of their choices or directions to turn is working effectively for them.

The simplest way to deal with this dilemma would be to meet with the husband to find out who in his life is he having an unsatisfying relationship with. Once he returns to being his "normal" self, his wife would have no need to react the way she has been and cases closed.

But her husband didn't call. She did. So I recommended she make an appointment to see me so that we could talk about what she can do to deal with his behavior that would be more effective for her than what she has been doing.

And if I can get them both to come and see me, then there is a better chance of resolving his issues too. After ruling out drugs/alcohol, we just might find that he is unhappy in his marriage.

Let's take this particular situation by the Choice Theory numbers:

1. Her husband is behaving in a way she disapproves of.
2. He is behaving in unfamiliar ways because of his own unhappiness.
3. Both individuals are frustrated because important people in their lives are behaving in unacceptable ways.
4. In her quality world, her husband does not behave the way he does
5. In his quality world, she is not living up to his image of how he wants his wife to behave. The result: Unhappiness.
6. They have both been using external control psychology and the Seven Deadly Sins on each other until all of the love and respect that they once had together is now hanging by a thread.
7. Nothing in their tool boxes have worked to resolve their unhappiness so he is acting strangely and she is reacting with physical pain. Both behaviors on each of their parts were created by them to deal with their frustration and inability to satisfy their basic needs.

How could this all be resolved? Either work with her and discover some possible alternative ways in dealing with her unhappiness and/or work with him and discover some possible things he might do to resolve his unhappiness, or work with both of them and save the marriage, if neither one has already decided to resort to divorce.

Is Addiction A Choice?

I don't know of anyone who said, "I think I'd like to become an addict" or "an alcoholic." Those are not aspirations that one would commonly choose to become due to the overall social negativity and the image it conveys. Nor does one choose to have diabetes, brain cancer, or any other number of medical illnesses that have pathology.

There are, however, certain illnesses that are acquired by the mere fact that an individual continued to do something that is known to be addictive. The greatest of these is the drug Nicotine which causes over 440,000–deaths a year. (NIDA 2006) We don't hear this statistic too often because most of the people who die as a result of smoking are listed as having other reasons for the cause of their death. Heart disease is one such disease. We see the words "heart disease" and perceive it as an illness of its own without associating the use of nicotine and smoking for a number of years to be the cause of it. The reason for this is that there is more than one way a person can acquire heart disease so it is used to label one illness and the specifier for its occurrence is omitted.

If you take a drug or any addictive substance and continue to take it knowing all along that it is a habit forming drug, is that not a choice? Years ago, there was an old wives tale devised to keep young men from masturbating. Young men were told, "If you keep that up, you'll go blind." From whence came the comic line from the young man, "I'll just do it until I need glasses." There exists a belief among users and drinkers that if one continues to use or drink and they start to see that they are becoming addicted, "I'll just stop before it gets to the point that I can't stop." The problem with this belief is: By the time one discovers

ction, it's already too late and they can't stop.
son they don't stop before it is too late is due to
..ice on the drug for sociological or psychological
.nich creates the dreaded "denial" that they have a
pro. ..m in the first place.

It is common knowledge that many drugs and alcohol are habit forming. But knowledge is information and information can not make you behave. You have a choice of many behaviors you can choose from once given the information. You can choose to use the drug or alcohol and take the risk of addiction. You can refuse to use the drug or alcohol and not have any risk. Or, you can choose to attempt to use the drug or alcohol until "you only need glasses." But addictions are not that simple. Once addicted, the addiction progresses.

People become addicted to substances at different times. Some become addicted the first time they drink or use. Others may drink or use for years before they cross the line to dependency. When does the use become addictive? It happens when you cannot seem to function without it or you rely on it to deal with the stressors in your life. You may feel sick and have all sorts of physical ailments such as sweating, hallucinating, irritability; the inability to sleep or to concentrate. You may feel severe aches and pains or even have seizures, all depending on what you have been putting in your body. Death is also a common symptom of dependency. When your liver ceases to function, all of your other internal organs shut down as well. Would you still want to drink or use drugs until you die just a little bit?

The fact is, by choosing to ignore the knowledge that you are taking an addictive substance, or, by continuing to use a substance that is causing you problems in your life and you continue to do so, you are choosing to become addicted.

You just don't believe that the addiction will happen to you and that you believe that you can control it before you do become addicted.

Your choice to drink or use is just that, a choice, but your addiction is not a choice. That's because alcohol is a legal drug and you didn't get addicted the first time you drank it. The first time you took any illegal drugs, you may not have become addicted either. This is why people continue to drink or use drugs. By the time they have become dependent on the substance, the greatest of all facets of addiction raises its ugly head and has such control over you that you listen to every word it tells you. It says, "You aren't addicted. Those people don't know what they're talking about. They just want to take away your happiness because they're jealous. Who are they to tell you that you have an addiction when they drink or use just as much as you do? They will all turn on you but I'll be with you for as long as you need me. They want to separate us. They have no idea how well you and I get along and how much we need each other. You're in complete control. They don't have a clue as to what they are talking about."

Once you begin to make excuses for your drinking or drug use, you're hooked. And you didn't choose to get hooked. You chose to use a drug that made all of your unwanted emotions and thoughts go away. You just wanted to feel better. You didn't want to have to think about all of those things that cause you to have unhappiness and unwanted physical reactions. The hook came when you weren't looking. Your body and brain decided that as long as you were going to continually use your drug of choice, it may as well learn how to deal with it on a regular basis. In other words, your body and brain adjusted to its presence. When you are not drinking or using, your body and brain will be the first to tell you that something, the drug, is missing and in order to feel better, they want you to give it to them.

Now you have a choice. If you choose not to use/drink, your body and brain will react violently and in varying degrees depending upon the severity of your addiction. Your body will begin to have withdrawal symptoms that are so uncomfortable and make you feel sick. Rather than continue to feel sick and uncomfortable, you choose to drink/drug and those unwanted reactions go away quite quickly. Incidentally, antidepressant drugs and other prescribed brain medications can have the same effect.

So back to the original question: Is addiction a choice? Yes. It's a choice to use/drink to overcome the illness and/or uncomfortable feelings you have when you are not drinking or using. You could also choose not to drink or drug but then you would have to undergo all of the withdrawal symptoms and misery that go with them. You will also have a floodgate of unwanted emotions and behaviors that are often embarrassing and painful. Which is easier to deal with . . . the addiction or the sobriety? The addict/alcoholic will always choose the addiction as the easier of the two.

Sobriety is hard, at first. There's nothing easy about it. But you must be willing to go through the pain and agony of losing something you've been using for years in order to cope and deal with all of your unmet basic needs and relationship conflicts. All you need is a better tool than what you've been using. There are places to go for medical detox should you have severe withdrawals. Medical supervision for some addicts and alcoholics works very well by the use of other medications to overcome the withdrawals. These medications, however, should not be used for more than 3 to 5 days and used only during time of detoxification.

For this next statement, you'll need to take my word for it. Not only have I personally experienced it but so have so many of those whom I have worked with over the years to deal with their addictions. The statement is: The "high" you will get from being clean and sober and from recovery is not only the ultimate "high," but it lasts a long time. And I hope that this is what you would prefer to have in your life instead of what you may currently have by dealing with your addiction.

Is Alcoholism A Disease?

Here is the part that will upset many of my associates and other professionals in the field of substance abuse and dependence. I contend that alcoholism was included as a disease by the AMA in an effort to take the stigma off of the problem in order to help those with the addiction to be more willing to seek help. The old way of looking at alcoholism, which also continues to exist in some circles today, is that alcoholism is a character disorder. I have even had alcoholics believe this to be true and this is one of the reasons they don't seek help and a major cause of their denial of their problem. Another reason that it was termed a "disease" was so that insurance companies could pay for treatment.

An August 1997 conference of International Doctors of Alcoholics survey reported that 80% of responding doctors see alcoholism as merely bad behavior while 90% of Americans believe it is a disease.[1] In the November 1995 issue of Lancet, Dr. Raoul Walsh contends that physicians have negative views about alcoholics based upon the empirical data showing physicians have stereotypical attitudes about alcoholics because most of their exposure to alcoholics is with late-stage dependence. (Same source as above)

Once addicted, there are physical things occurring in the body. For those of you who recall the first time you inhaled a cigarette, how did you body react? You most likely coughed your fool head off. That was your brain that recognized you had just put something in your lungs and

---

[1] (Source: Managing Alcoholism as a disease,
http://www.physiciansnews.com/commentary/298wp.html)

blood that doesn't belong there. The brain triggered a response for you to cough to eliminate the smoke from your lungs. Those of you who continued to inhale caused your brain to give up sending the message because you continued to not listen to your brain telling you to stop.

The same thing happens when we drink or use other drugs. The brain tells you that this is not normal and fights against it while you continue to use and eventually, the brain gives up and says, "Screw it." He's going to continue to drink (or use) no matter what I say so I'm just going to shut up. And then, to help the brain keep its comments to itself, certain cells in your body begin to adjust to deal with the drug or the alcohol. When the body does not receive the drug or the alcohol, it cries out in the form of withdrawal symptoms to tell you to put it in your body so that they can go back to feeling comfortable. The addict or alcoholic only feels sick when s/he is not drinking our using. They feel better and even to some stages of "normal" when they are drinking or using.

In the realm of our legal system, whatever a person believes doesn't matter. What does matter is what one can prove. So far, the disease concept that alcoholism is, in fact, a pathological disease has never been proven. In all of my personal research, those who take the stand of alcoholism being a disease always end up returning to the subjective approach of observing behavior to prove their point.

Yes, we can predict specific behaviors when one is under the influence. Yes, we can predict what will happen if they don't stop drinking or using. Yes, we can see physical evidence of what alcohol and drugs can and will do to the body. Regarding these predictions and observations is the fact that what we are observing and predicting is the result of drinking and using, not the *cause* of addiction. The damage done from drinking and using is a cause of drinking and using but not why they are addicted.

I have had people in the medical field, those who don't even work with addicts or alcoholics want to argue their point by citing some M.R.I. (Magnetic Resonance Imaging) findings somewhere that indicated those who were alcoholics had either something showing up or something missing in the M.R.I. that non-addicts or non-alcoholics do or don't have. Again, any images of the brain can only show brain activity or the lack of it. It was this sort of reasoning that led the way for Select Serotonin Reuptake Inhibitors (SSRIs) and other anti-depressant drugs to permeate society as a cure-all for depression . . . another so-called mental illness with no pathology. Does a person who is always depressing do so because of a chemical imbalance of not enough serotonin? If so, then someone who is always happy must have an abundance of dopamine. So why not medicate depression with massive doses of dopamine? Because it would be the same thing as saying one has a history of headaches because they don't have enough aspirin in their brain.

According to the DSMIV, you have a mental illness if you are:
Addicted to caffeine
Addicted to or abuse of hallucinogens
Addicted to Nicotine
Addicted to or abuse of Sedatives
Addicted to gambling
Addicted to or abuse of inhalants
Addicted to sex
Addicted to or abuse of Amphetamine
Addicted to or abuse of alcohol
Addicted to or abuse of cocaine

Addicted to or abuse of opiates
Addicted to or abuse of Cannabis

In fact, on page 50 and 51 of the DSM IV, you have a mental illness if your math skills fall below that expected for your age. It doesn't matter whether or not you simply don't like mathematics. The same diagnosis of mental illness applies to those whose writing skills fall below those expected of their age. These mental illnesses are called: Mathematics Disorder with an Axis I code of 315.1, and Disorder of Written Expression with an Axis I code of 315.2

Of all of the so-called mental illness listed above, as well as over 200 other mental illnesses listed in the DSM IV, not a one of them have any laboratory tests to indicate their cause. These diagnoses are made strictly by observation of one's behavior(s) and no pathology for any of them exists. There are lab tests to prove if many of the substances listed are in one's body but none to prove the actual cause of their addiction.

So if what can be proven is necessary to hold evidence of fact, then what is proven is that neither the American Psychiatric Association (APA) nor the National Institute of Mental Health (NIMH) nor any other medical organization can provide today any scientific evidence to prove that any psychiatric disorder is an <u>Objective, Confirmable, Abnormality</u> of the brain.

When A.A. cofounder Bill Wilson was asked in 1960 about A.A.'s position on the disease concept, he offered the following:
　　"We have never called alcoholism a disease because, technically speaking, it is not a disease entity. For example, there is no such thing as heart disease.

Instead, there are many separate heart ailments, or combinations of them. It is something like that with alcoholism. Therefore, we did not wish to get in wrong with the medical profession by pronouncing alcoholism a disease entity. Therefore, we always called it an illness, or a malady, a far safer term for us to use.[2]*"*

The disease model of addiction is credited to E.M. Jellinek in 1960. The World Health Organization acknowledged alcoholism as a medical problem in 1951. The AMA declared alcoholism as a treatable illness in 1956 and then the American Psychiatric Association decided to use the term "disease" for alcoholism in 1965. The American Medical Association then jumped on the band wagon in 1966[3].

The above source also reports that Jellinek's data were gathered "from questionnaires that were distributed to A.A. members through its newsletter, "The Grapevine." Of 158 questionnaires returned, 60 were discarded because members had pooled and averaged their responses and no questionnaires from women were used. Jellinek himself acknowledged that his data was limited. Therefore, one might wonder why Jellinek's concept of the disease of alcoholism received such widespread acceptance."

If alcoholism and other drug addictions are diseases with scientific and medical pathology, how is it that I, who am not a doctor, have a license to treat individuals with substance dependence? If alcoholism is a medical disease, where are all of the medications that the pharmaceutical companies would be jumping on and touting as a cure for

---

[2] White, W. (2000) The Rebirth of the Disease Concept of Alcoholism in the 20th Century. Counselor, 1(2):62-66

[3] Source: http://www.alcohol-drug-treatment.net/disease.html

it? They have medications for all of the other so-called mental illnesses. The DSM IV lists alcoholism as a mental illness.

There are only three drugs that are being used today in the so-called "treatment" of alcoholism. Those drugs are: Disulfiram (antabuse), Daltrexone (also known as Revia or Depade), and Acamprosate or Campral. These drugs are prescribed by doctors and psychiatrists but not by counselors or therapists who are not doctors. Those doctors who administer these medications can not tell you how they work just as they can not tell you how anti-depressants work. But they will still give the same rhetoric that it works by restoring a "chemical imbalance" in your brain. There is not and never has been to date any way to test a "chemical imbalance" in a person's brain.

These drugs do not cure alcoholism. Naltrexone is used to treat the symptoms of withdrawal other than cravings. Disulfiram does not treat any withdrawal symptoms or stop cravings. It inhibits the liver's ability to metabolize acetaldehyde, a chemical change of alcohol when it first passes through the liver. While on this drug, one gets violently ill if drinking alcohol. Several years ago, this drug caused many deaths due to liver and kidney damage caused by the alcoholic's determination to continue drinking in spite of its ill effects. The last drug, Acamprosate, serves to reduce the physical and emotional stress experienced by those who are abstaining. It has been used more often in Europe than in America because American medical detox practitioners have relied on valium and other sedatives to do the job that Acamprosate is reported to do.

Alcoholism has been called a progressive disease that moves through stages. Again, the stages they refer to are behaviors performed by the person who is addicted and not by any pathology. The closest anyone has come to providing a scientific explanation of alcoholism by Dr. David L Ohlms in his book the Disease Concept of Alcoholism.

Dr. Ohlms reported that when the liver first attempts to metabolize alcohol from the body, it turns it into something called acetaldehyde, a form of formaldehyde, which is very toxic and poisonous to the body. After the acetaldehyde has made the second trip throughout the drinker's body, through every cell and organ in the body, it comes to the liver a second time and the liver must change the acetaldehyde into two other chemical changes on two more subsequent trips. But before the acetaldehyde gets to the liver the second time, another chemical change occurs in the brain of those who have been drinking long enough and hard enough. In these individuals, the acetaldehyde creates a chemical in their brain known as THIQ for short (actually called Tetrahydroisoquinoline)

There is an interesting story that goes along with the discovery of this chemical THIQ and you can read it by going to Google and typing "THIQ." According to the research that was conducted on THIQ, it is what causes one to drink in spite of the bad taste and in spite of all of the trouble it causes an alcoholic. It was first discovered in the brains of heroin addicts. The chemical has much of the same properties as morphine. And once contracted, it lasts forever, which would explain the only cure for alcoholism is total abstinence. It doesn't go away just because the drinker quits drinking.

The compelling evidence of a disease was after rats that refuse to drink anything that contains alcohol, began to literally drink themselves to death once given a tiny injection in their brains of THIQ. This is not a new discovery. It has been around for years and one that I have, on occasion, used in my lectures on the effects of alcohol on the body and the brain. However, it comes and goes in and out of favor in the scientific and medical realms of research. One of the reasons for losing favor being that the rats were injected with the THIQ rather than having developed it on their own like an alcoholic would have through his years of drinking. But even an alcoholic would never take THIQ itself in its pure form because it is some very foul smelling stuff. The alcoholic gets it from drinking alcohol on his own volition, something the rats won't do and after the liver turns it into acetaldehyde, the acetaldehyde creates the THIQ.

You would think that the medical profession would be quick to jump on this theory in order to help prove their point and position on the disease concept. Ironically, they are the ones who continually try to debunk it.

But if THIQ is responsible for the addiction to alcohol, what is responsible for the addiction to all of the other substances and behaviors listed in the DSM IV? What chemical or chemical imbalance makes a person a compulsive gambler, sex addict, workaholic, spender, coffee drinker, poor math skills, and the inability to have writing skills? While the last two examples are not addictions, the idea that they are mental illnesses or medical condition is as inane as saying addictions are mental illnesses or medical conditions.

Whether or not alcoholism is a disease or not, it has absolutely no effect on how we are treating it. Doctors are not providing a cure through medicine and counselors are not providing help through doctoring. But one thing one can be assured of. It is not a mental illness. The behaviors that are observed as being "mental" are no more than the normal behavior of someone whose brain is affected by drugs. Once the drug is eliminated from the brain, the "mental illness" behaviors will cease. What follows will be the need for learning new behaviors to deal with unhappiness.

Is Alcoholism Genetic?

I'm going to upset some more of my associates and fellow substance abuse therapists. They, like me, were all trained in the medical model of therapy. In the Chicago Tribune dated 3/20/2001: "It is a fact that despite decades of research, not a single gene responsible for mental illness has been found – the quest has been shattered by the debunking of highly visible reports localizing genes for schizophrenia,. Similar fates met discoveries of genes for manic-depression, alcoholism, and homosexuality." Gorner (2001)

I don't know if alcoholism is genetic or not. So far, no gene has been identified for anyone to make the claim of genetic predispositions. So currently, the answer is no, it is not genetic.

Is Alcoholism environmental?

There's a real good chance that much of alcoholism and drug addiction is environmental. We know that it is quite common for some people to deal with stress the same way their parents did. There could be any number of different behaviors but alcohol and drug use is clearly included. Just because one or more parent used to drink or drug to deal with stress does not mean that all of their offspring will do so. However, learned behavior is a known part of our behavioral makeup.

Mark grew up in a family where his parents only drank socially at best. In fact, the primary caregiver, his mother, drank even less than socially. Mark had three other siblings, all of whom were affected by alcoholism. His sister, Carol, married a hardcore alcoholic. Mark was an alcoholic. His brother Daniel was an alcoholic and drug user, and his youngest brother, Harlan, was addicted to cocaine and abused alcohol. How could this be so to parents who did not display any behaviors of abuse or addiction? Many would respond, "Genetics." But they would be wrong.

Their mother was a strong influence in her children's lives. Their father was away much of the time and had left all of the childrearing duties to his wife. She had grown up in an alcoholic family. Her father was the town drunk, something she would deny all of her life. Both she and her brother grew up in an alcoholic environment, including all of the horrid things that can go with living with such a family. There was infidelity going on in her family, arguments, yelling, destroyed property, and even incest behind closed doors of her family. Mark's mother, Jane, grew up frightened, ashamed, embarrassed, ridden with guilt, and would compensate for all of her unwanted emotions and behaviors of her father by overachieving.

While in school, Jane went to no expense to make sure that she was a straight A student. She had to really work at it too. She belonged to as many school organizations that she could join and even held office in most of them. She was voted the schools most popular girl. While all of this was occurring outside of the home, inside the home was different story. Jane never dated in school because her father forbade it. She had lots of friends at school but never, ever did she invite any of them to her home. Jane's motivation was first and foremost, "to look good in the public's eye." While the town may talk about her alcoholic father, it was her intent to shine and overcompensate for his imperfections by being a star . . . an outstanding person. In doing so, who could say anything bad about her family? At least, that was her reasoning. She had no social skills. She was filled with shame and guilt.

When Jane got married, she had sexual problems relating to her fear of sex. She suffered from what would be called Irritable Bowel Syndrome today as well as several migraine headaches for several years of her marriage. When she gave birth to her first child, she didn't know how to be a healthy mother. She was filled with anxiety, fear, and depression. Her first child could sense this negative energy and would incessantly cry for love, attention, and comfort, something Jane was short on in supply. Jane was told by her doctor that the child had colic. Meanwhile, Jane could hardly deal with her child's constant crying. She perceived herself as being an unfit mother and would only pile more shame and guilt on herself which only added more negative emotions and unhappiness that she would convey to her infant.

Mark reports that he had been told that when he was born, his mother used to have to wake him in order to feed him. He was very laid back and content as long as he was fed and asleep. Conflict was the last thing he ever wanted to see or experience. He grew up timid and a loner, also with little to no social skills. Their third child, Daniel, was premature and born with a slight heart condition. It would not be surprising that this premature birth was also the result of Jane's own unhappiness. Daniel not only became a hardcore drinker, he also married a woman whose parents were alcoholics. The fourth born child came several years later. He would grow up at a time when the family was going through their own hard emotional times and he was often passed off to another woman to care for him while Jane was now working out of the home. Harlan grew up with a gender identity problem and was only comfortable when he could create chaos all around him . . . at his family's expense. Harlan wanted fraternity with his other siblings, but with the exception of Daniel, the other siblings were either much older or even out of the house to have any affiliation with him except during holidays.

Their mother raised the children to "always look good." The message given was "what goes on behind closed doors in this family is no body's business so keep your mouth shut." The madness of all of this was that they didn't know what it was that they were not supposed to talk about. Trust was something that was not only not to be given outside of the home; it wasn't to be given within the family either. Placing guilt on her children if they disobeyed, or if they didn't do what Jane wanted them to do, was her parenting technique. She would also punish by not talking to any of them whom she felt did wrong. Emotional abandonment was her form of parenting and setting guidelines. The children were taught three major rules: Don't talk, don't trust, and don't feel. Jane had no boundaries, herself. She would go through her children's personal things, read their personal mail, pile feelings of guilt and shame on them when they behaved in ways in which she disapproved. There was no bathroom privacy etiquette. If the bathroom was being used and someone else needed it for other things, just go right in. Jane also had the habit of walking around the house between the bathroom and her bedroom nude with the doors open. Manipulation to get others to do things was very common and usually consisted of some form of guilt if the other party was reluctant to do it. Jane also was adept at taking just a little tiny bit of information and coming to a major unchecked assumable conclusion which would always be wrong. Then she would punish by guilt, "you obviously don't love or respect me for you to do things like that." She would not listen to the fact that she was wrong. In her mind, her conclusions were always right.

For the first 12 or 13 years of their life, Mark and his siblings grew up in a nuclear bubble limited only to the family unit, parochial school, and occasional outside areas that would be accompanied by the parent(s). But somewhere around Jr. High School age, the older siblings began to realize that there is another world out there and one of which they were and will be a part of. They began to compare themselves to others; checking their behavior compared to the behavior of others; looking to see if they measure up to their peers; if they were accepted by others; and checking to see how others see and feel about them.

Mark stated, "At first, I thought I was messed up because I was behaving a lot differently than everyone else around me. But then, I came to the conclusion that it wasn't me, it was everyone else who was messed up." Still, he reported that he was shy and uncertain around others. He remembered that he wasn't supposed to talk and he was afraid that anything he might say to someone else might be what he wasn't supposed to talk about. He reports he lived like this all through high school and up to the age of 21 when he first was old enough to go to a bar. He said, "The first time I ever went into a bar, I just found the rest of my family." He related that everyone he would meet in a bar felt and behaved the way he did and he felt right at home for the first time in his life. Bars would go on to become his living room in the future.

So in Mark's family, we can say that environment and nurture were the reasons why four out of four children became involved in dependence as the result of growing up in an alcoholic environment even though alcohol was not there. Jane had passed along all of the ways she was brought up in an alcoholic world to her children. Jane's passing along her knowledge to her children in how to live in an alcoholic family would not appear to be problematic until the children turned into teens and saw how they were different than others, and how it would all come together and make sense for them once they began drinking, using, or being with other alcoholics. Nothing they had learned from their mother made sense until they got around alcohol or drugs.

It makes no difference if your addiction is genetic or environmental. The only thing that matters is that you overcome your addiction. Knowing why you are addicted won't change a darn thing until you take measures to take responsibility for your own behavior, create meaningful relationships, and get back control of your life.

Is Alcoholism the Result of Past Trauma?

If you watch any of the Intervention programs on television or listen to the psychiatric community and people on the street, "The cause of his/her addiction is because s/he was sexually abused as a child," or "they were physically abused," etc, etc.

People are not addicts because of past problems in their lives. The problems of the past are why they started to drink. They consumed an addictive substance to deal with their present unhappiness at the time. The problems they had in the past are over and done with. Addicts are not consumed with problems that no longer exist. They are consumed by the addiction to the substance and the current problems the addiction is causing now . . . problems that are occurring at this moment in time. Many of the problems faced by addicts and alcoholics go away or are resolved once they become clean and sober. What happens next is a period of restructuring --a learning process to acquire what they failed to acquire normally during maturation such as: how to find more effective ways of dealing with adversity, identifying emotions and what those emotions mean, and how to live with others in as much of a conflict-free manner as possible, the latter being difficult even for those who do not have any addictions.

What Causes Addiction?

The causes of substance addiction are simple: "The continued use of an addictive substance." That's it. There is nothing fancy or complex about it. If you are addicted, you have been using an addictive substance.

Now if you want to know why you would take an addictive substance, would this help you become un-addicted? No. Knowledge of causes does not dissipate the addiction. Knowing why you drink or use will only explain why you drink or use. The addict or alcoholic first becomes addicted by drinking or using to cover up their unwanted emotions of what or who they have not become in their life. Later in their addiction, they will be drinking/using to cover up their unwanted emotions of what they indeed have become. They will drink or use even more when others are behaving in ways in which they disapprove.

You are addicted because:

1. **Your use serves to meet sociological needs**.

None of us began drinking or using alone. We all started out in a social type setting. Over our continued use, we forget about the bad times it causes, remember only the good times we had, and then we rely on it for that purpose. Some may say, "it's fun," or "I feel more confident around others when I drink (or use)." No one ever relates to others how much fun they had getting their DUI, fighting with their family or friends, getting sick and vomiting, spending all their money on drugs, having hangovers, losing jobs, family, and friends. This is why we tend to hang out with other drinkers/users. They can relate. Normies can not.

2. **Your use serves to meet psychological needs**.

Since all of our behavior serves to meet one or more of our genetic needs (specifically: happiness), we have come to discover that when we are worried, feel shameful, feel guilty, lack confidence and self-worth, alcohol and drugs do a wonderful job of making these unwanted thoughts and emotions go away albeit temporarily. The only way to maintain the absence of these unwanted emotions is to continue to drink/use. We also drink to deal with the frustration of the unwanted behavior of others who are important to us.

3. **Your use serves to meet your physiological needs**.

Your body has become accustomed to an addictive substance and when you don't take the drug, your body reacts negatively . . . screaming at you to take it because many of your body's cells are violently reacting for the want of the drug. Once you begin to take the drug, your body calms down and settles as the drug takes effect.

So now that you have that bit of information, does that make you want to quit? Of course not. Any one of these causes for addiction or abuse is difficult to overcome. The more of them you possess the more difficult and harder you will need to work to overcome them. Impossible you say? Naw. Hundreds of thousands of people have overcome their addictions and have found more happiness and peace of mind than they ever encountered. So can you.

If you have ever been intoxicated, as most have at one time or another, you are able to recall not only the event but some of the things that happened while intoxicated. Even when drunk, we can recall some of the things we were doing. I often ask clients why they drink alcohol and many of them say, "To have fun." While the liver fights to get alcohol out of your body, the pleasure centers of the brain fool you into believing you are enjoying the experience. However, continued use of the drug eventually causes the brain to not react to the pleasure. In other words, the pleasure of drinking begins to disappear. When this happens, you require more of the drug. If you find yourself drinking the first few drinks quickly, you are not drinking it for "the enjoyment of the taste." You are gulping your drinks to get the effect or feeling of pleasure. You are addicted and the brain is no longer functioning as it should.

This same process occurs with other drugs as well. The body and brain increase in tolerance of the drug and you find yourself having to take more of the drug than you used to in order to get the effects you want.

If you have a high tolerance to alcohol, you are not a normal drinker. How many drinks can you have before you feel their effect? If you said one or two, that would be normal. If you said three or four, that would indicate an increase in tolerance. If you said, "I can drink 5 or 6 drinks before I get a buzz," you are A) either addicted or B) about to become addicted.

A drinkers "buzz" is his sweetheart. It is his body telling him that it's time to ease up or back off a little on his consumption. Even though he may be clearly drunk, the buzz is his most important drinking companion. He has learned over the years to rely on the buzz to keep him from going "too far" in situations where he needs not to go too far. But in time, anyone who drinks long enough and hard enough will lose their buzz. They then go from sober to drunk without any warning whatsoever and wake up on the floor asking, "What the hell happened?"

Does the buzz come back after periods of abstinence? I have yet to find or hear an alcoholic tell me that it returns. Several have reported to me that they tested to see if they "got their buzz back" only to find out that they didn't and only succeeded in relapsing and getting falling down drunk. This is another reason why we say that the only cure for alcoholism is total abstinence.

In several of my experiences, I have seen clients who were addicted to prescription drugs such as valium lose the effect the drug had on them without taking exorbitant amounts of the drug. I am truly amazed when I find out that some of the doctors of these individuals either switch to another addictive drug or even increase the dosage, further supporting their addiction.

Some doctors are so sympathetic of their clients' aches and pain that all they do is worry about how they can save their patients from their pain. In so doing, they don't even recognize the addicting aspects of the drug and either increase the dosage or prescribe a stronger drug in the same class. I have had some clients tell me that their doctors have told them that the physical effects they are experiencing when they run out of the drug is actually "a relapse" of the condition in which they were prescribed the drug in the first place.

A very recent client of mine came to see me to get evaluated to see if he was safe to get his driver's license reinstated after having an alcohol DUI, a prescription drug DUI, and an arrest for paraphernalia and possession of Cannabis. He has a bad back and went to our local pain clinic. He informed the doctors of his past chronic addiction to alcohol and drugs yet they prescribed him 30 mg of OxyCodone, a highly addictive drug, and had him sign a release that would keep the doctors not responsible and not liable should he abuse or become dependent on the medication. Why not throw gasoline on a burning man?

Instead of looking into the client's current unhappiness, the medical person will often only look at the physical aspects of a client . . . disregarding the mental health issues, or the patient's unhappiness that may be leading to the patient's aches and pains. If they do recognize some mental health issues, they place the patient on brain medications that only cover up the symptoms, have no curative powers, and cause another addiction to another drug.

To those who are addicted to either drugs or alcohol, there is little anyone is willing to do to overcome the addiction for the sake of the pleasure that the drug or alcohol gives them. This is why it is so difficult for people to overcome their substance addictions. The pleasure received far outweighs the agony of withdrawal symptoms.

What Causes Low Self-Esteem, Shame, & Guilt?

There are several possible causes of low self-esteem, shame and guilt. Criticism during your formative years is a leading factor. Constant complaining or blaming you for anything that goes wrong in your family is yet another cause. All of these things happen early in life. There is no later onset of low self-esteem and low self-worth. Physical punishment, threats of punishment or abandonment also contribute to low self-worth. Constant nagging lowers self-worth and instills shame and guilt. A parent or parents who possess low self-worth, shame and guilt have a tendency to instill these same feelings and perceptions in their own children without realizing they are doing it. But of all the possible causes, the one that is perhaps the most powerful in instilling low self-esteem and shame and guilt is your own perception of yourself, aided and abetted by what others in your life have told you what you are.

Here's the good part. It doesn't matter how or why you have low self-worth, and shame, and guilt. What matters is what you do to rise above it. Knowledge of causes will not change your life for the better. Whatever happened to you in the past is just that . . . the past. You can not change anything that happened to you in the past including any thoughts that you may have had in the last 10 seconds.

To continue to look at the past; to blame whatever may have happened to you (both real and/or imagined) on other people; to dwell on past circumstances will do absolutely nothing except to make you feel like "a victim" and keep you from rising above whatever it is that led to your shame, guilt, and low self-esteem. As a matter of fact, staying in the past will only reinforce your negative thoughts and keep you stuck in these unwanted feelings about yourself. In essence, staying stuck in the past only gives you an excuse not to do the things you need to do to rise above them and take control of your life. Staying stuck in the past gives you an excuse to keep you from doing what you know you need to do to help yourself that will lead to giving you the life that you ultimately want to have. Staying stuck in the past is also a way of keeping others in your life feeling sorry for you for all that you went through . . . it brings you attention and people to feel sorry of you.

There are many people in the psychiatric delivery system who seek out your past sorrows and hurts. The idea behind this is that these are "core issues" that are contributing to all of your misery and troubles in your life because they believe that you keep thinking about them either consciously or unconsciously. They are partially correct. You may continue to think about past events and thinking about past hurts and trauma. But these thoughts will only create present hurts and present sorrows. If you go back in your past and bring up old hurts and wounds, you will leave the therapist's office feeling worse than you did when you first got there. Little is done to relive the past except to get you to hurt. You can not make improvements in your life when thinking of hurtful thoughts. Just see how successful you are taking positive action and control of your life the next time you stub your bare toe on a piece of furniture.

The general idea of those therapists who want to take you back into the past and get you to recall your past hurts and trauma appears to be, "If you don't resolve these past issues, you won't get any better or find happiness." Since we can't change whatever has happened in the past, the only thing one can do about the past is to accept it and get on with your life. Rather than look for the bad that may have come of your past, what good came of your bad experiences. I can tell you that I would never have become a therapist had I not become addicted to alcohol.

Does rehashing or thinking about past injustice or abuse bring you happiness or unhappiness? Does reliving these past experiences in your mind and discussing them with a therapist or someone else change what has happened to you? While you may acquire insight as to why it occurred and the effect it may have had on you, did this insight lead to any change in your life and bring you closer to those things that you want?

Our society, therapists, clergy, police officers, and doctors are often the cause of creating more trauma and emotional pain than a person may have originally experienced merely by their own attitudes about the event. Murder is viewed by most people as terrible but pedophilia and rape is perceived as the worst of the worse. They often tell the victim that they have been violated more than they could ever be violated and will bear the trauma of the experience for the rest of their life. What we experience does, indeed, play a major role in whom and what we are but it does not have to all be negative.

Some of the greatest individuals of all time experienced very difficult times and experiences. Not all victims of crime or hardship are affected in ways that will keep them suppressed or oppressed. To some victims, it is the things that happened to them that caused them to rise above whatever occurred to them and brought them success and happiness. Why can some achieve this and others not? It appears to be based upon how they choose to perceive whatever it is that happened to them.

It just doesn't matter what has happened to you in the past. You can't change one iota of that unfortunate experience in your life. What *does* matter is how you react to the things that have happened in your life as well as whatever tools you have acquired over the years to deal with them in a beneficial manner rather than an unhealthy way of dealing with them.

To improve your self-worth, you will need to compare and self-evaluate between the real world and your quality world. If your self-worth is low, you perceive yourself in the real world differently than you are in your quality world. The mind does not know the difference between fact and fiction. It will believe whatever you put into it.

For several hundred years, it was generally thought that the world was flat. It was also generally believed that man could never run a mile in less than four minutes. If man wanted to fly, God would have given him wings, etc. Man will never go to the moon. These and many thoughts just like them were beliefs held by most of the world at one time or another. By updating the information, we know them all to be false statements. The mind will believe whatever you tell it.

So how much of how and what you see in yourself is true? Is it possible that what others have been saying about you over the years is false? Is it also possible that some of what others have said is true? How much have you been living up to the perceptions of other people? How much of your alcohol and drug use is the result of living up to what others have said about you. I mean, if others have identified you and described you in certain negative values, could your use of drugs or alcohol be your way of becoming what they have been saying about you all of this time? Is it possible that their perceptions were wrong from the get-go and all that you have been doing is proving them right?

How do you see yourself? Is your perception of yourself a lot different now than it was before you started drinking or using? Did your use of drugs or alcohol improve your self image or did it make it worse? How would you like to see yourself? If you were to take a photograph of yourself that depicted how you would really like to appear to yourself and to others, what would the picture look like? How would the photo be different than the way you appear to yourself and others today?

Since you are the only one who can control you, what are some of the things that you can do to live up to the image of the photo that you would prefer? How many truly successful and happy people do you know who are addicted to drugs or alcohol? How many famous people can you name, from the past, who lost all that they had, including their life, due to drugs and alcohol? What kind of future do you see for yourself if you continue to use drugs or alcohol?

The images we have in our quality world are always changing and they may not necessarily be factual as to their existence. Have you ever wanted something in your life that you wanted more than anything else in the world and when you finally got it, it wasn't all what you expected it to be? In your quality world, you had the picture of the item or thing or person that would make you happy only to find out that it didn't pan out.

Perhaps one of the best ways to describe this situation is any time you got involved in a relationship or got married. The other person you placed in your quality world was everything you ever wanted. You were happy as you could possibly be for the first few months or years.

But then something happened. One or the other of you, and eventually both of you, began using the seven deadly habits on one another. Respect and love for each other was slowly being destroyed by the deadly habits. And then . . . the image you once had of one another changed and you took each other out of your quality worlds.

It was totally voluntary and your choice to see the other person differently and to change them in your quality world . . . all because they were behaving in a way that you disapproved. If either of you had chosen not to treat one or the other with disdain and use the seven deadly habits, your positive image of them would still have remained in your quality world and the marriage or relationship would not have ended.

How you see yourself, your self image can be whatever you want it to be. You've been doing it all along by seeing yourself as not an addict or an alcoholic but the real world image depicts otherwise. In other words, do a reality check. What is real as opposed to what is fantasy? Reality has a way of screwing up an addict's fantasy.

If you don't like what you see, then do something about it to change the image. There is what we refer to in my group sessions as a shame and guilt spiral. The alcoholic already feels badly about himself because of all of the things he's done to himself and others over his years of drinking. He sees himself as a loser. He sees himself as someone who has something wrong with him. So he gets drunk and every one of those negative images he has of himself disappeared. That's why he drinks or uses in the first place. Then he sobers up and feels badly for getting drunk. "Cripes. Why did I get drunk again? I'm worthless and a loser." He's just piled on another 4 pounds of shame and guilt to carry around. So he drinks again so he doesn't have to admit or feel the way he does about himself and the downward spiral continues.

If you know what happy and successful people do in order to be happy and successful, what is keeping your from doing those things? Don't blame anyone else for your not doing them. It isn't anyone else's responsibility at this stage of your life to improve your self image and/or to cause you to be happy. It all must come from you because you are the only who can control you. The only way you can find happiness is to find different ways to relate to yourself and to others.

The more you drink or use drugs, the more you will cause others to see you in a negative light and more and more people will take you out of their quality world. Pretty soon, you're all you have left. Loneliness is a major excuse to drink or use drugs. They make you feel better and not think about what you don't have. So now we have another downward spiral.

Pleasure versus Happiness

The addict/alcoholic gets all of his basic needs met via his drug of choice. The problem, however, is that they are being fooled into believing that they are receiving happiness when, at best, all they are getting is temporary pleasure. Drugs and alcohol go to the pleasure center of the brain and fool the user into thinking that what they are experiencing is happiness. It does this by interfering with the part of the brain that causes them to worry or be upset with those things in life that they feel are causing them unhappiness. When your worries and fears go away, you naturally feel better. But this is not happiness. It's only temporary pleasure --a release from worries via an intense high from drugs, alcohol, sex, or gambling.

Pleasure is more intense than happiness. Happiness, on the other hand, lasts much longer than pleasure. Given the choice, the addict/alcoholic will choose pleasure over happiness any day because it is instant, much more intense, and they don't have to work at it. So what if it doesn't last long? They'll just do the behavior again, and again, and again. **That's the addiction!** The addict/alcoholic has no concept of the benefit of long term happiness over short term pleasure. To get from happiness instead of pleasure is not instant. It will take time. It is too frightening what will happen during the time it takes to find happiness and they don't know what to expect if they do find happiness. They know what to expect by staying with pleasure and it comes quickly.

What would you rather experience, feeling sick and miserable or feeling like nothing else you've ever felt that brings you pleasure? The addict/alcoholic will choose the latter even if they have to do it often to try to keep it going.

If the question were asked, what would you rather experience, feeling sick and miserable periodically several times a day or long term happiness with no more illness and misery, the addict may tell you he would choose long term happiness until he discovers that he feels sick and miserable for a few days and has a lot of other emotions come at him like a freight train that he didn't have until he quit drinking or using. While these results are only temporary, the addict/alcoholic often goes back to what he knows and can rely on, temporary relief.

It isn't always drugs or alcohol that fools one into believing they are experiencing happiness. One of my long-time friends, whom I shall call Larry, was experiencing tremendous grief. His wife had recently died from an incurable illness. His grief was justifiable. If someone close to you dies, and you don't experience the loss and not grieve over the loss, you might want to check your pulse for vital signs.

Larry was a power driven person in sales. He lost interest in his work and could do little except to feel the loss of his wife of over 30 some years. Larry lived over 2000 miles away from me but we kept in touch daily via phone or internet. Being a friend, I could not offer any therapy other than to share his loss with him and to be there for him whenever he needed to talk.

Larry had high basic needs for power, love, and acceptance. When his wife died, he felt he had even less because she was the only one in his mind who "truly understood" his needs. Larry was always planning things, things that were challenging. If he won, then he felt he had self-worth.

After approximately a year of mourning his wife's death, Larry decided that he needed to get involved with other women. It started out as what is often referred to as "mercy encounters." Larry only wanted to feel better and did not want to get involved in a meaningful relationship. He only wanted to stop the pain of his grief. Using sex as a tool to bring about what he wanted, happiness, he did not understand that there is a difference between happiness and pleasure. His sexual encounters would only bring him pleasure, which he began to rely on to feel better. The fact that another person would become sexually involved with him also boosted his self-worth --sex being, in his perception, the ultimate acceptance from another person and the proof of his power over someone else. Since pleasure is only short-lived, he found out that this was not doing what he wanted it to do. It was only effective in his world as long as he was involved.

Larry then began associating with younger women of 18 to 21 years of age. Where he lived, there were girls including those from other countries who would come to America to work in the resort areas, where Larry lived. One of the things Larry stated that he liked so much about his late wife was that she was accustomed to his "out there" ideas and would always go along with him rather than criticize him or put him down. He had come to the conclusion that older women were easy prey for his sexual conquests. He had become addicted to sex and the purpose of sex was not to be for love, but to give him pleasure, and self-worth for being able to seduce young women. He referred to it as "catch and release." He loved the game, he loved the conquest. It was his addiction. It afforded him the ability to detach and avoid intimate relationships.

Older women to Larry were not a challenge. Nor were they as naïve and inexperienced with dealing with someone whose ulterior motives were to use them for his own selfish needs. Younger women were more difficult to conquer and a challenge in the fact that while in his sixties, he could seduce them into bed. Larry was only fooling himself into thinking that his behaviors were bringing him happiness. At best, it only brought him pleasure that didn't last long and he would have to spend lots of time with the younger women to maintain relationships with them. Some were able to see through his ploy and tell him that they were not a toy. But this would only cause Larry to work harder to woo some other unsuspecting victim. Larry had no intentions whatsoever of ever hurting any of these young women. He was only selfishly concerned about his own need to satisfy his pleasure instead of finding happiness in meaningful relationships.

Added to Larry's sexual quests were other behaviors he would utilize that only had the effect of short-lived pleasure. He bought a $40,000 boat. He purchased an Excalibur auto. He also bought a top of the line motorcycle. He acquired a Jeep Wrangler, a new Chrysler 300. These material items are what he thought would bring him happiness (again confusing happiness with pleasure). He would use them to flaunt in public to impress others, especially the young girls.

Being power driven, Larry loved the challenge in business of closing sales as well as closing sexual encounters in his personal life. "Catch and release" does not allow for quality time together. Catching a younger person 40 years his junior was ego-satisfying but only afforded pleasure, not happiness. Larry's life was empty --void of happiness yet he would try to convince others otherwise. He would think about suicide but not take any direct action to make it a reality. His thoughts were, "I'm just biding my time until I die and hoping it will come sooner than later." These are not the thoughts of a happy person. If challenged about his macro suicidal ideations, he would say, "I'm not depressed.

I smile and laugh a lot." To Larry, this means he isn't depressing.

It is far more common for someone to resort to drugs or alcohol than to deal with the loss of a loved one. Larry was more creative than that. He chose to use the challenge of sexual conquests and the acquisition of material items to boost his low self-esteem and self-worth. In Larry's quality world, he thinks he is finding happiness. The reality of it is, Larry is unhappy and trying to convince himself that pleasure is happiness. He refuses to even attempt to get involved in a meaningful relationship; therefore, he is insuring his continuation of unhappiness. It would not surprise me that he may, indeed, take a more serious look at suicide. But even if he did, he would plan it to look like it was anything but suicide. Larry merely has a strong need for power in the form of attention. His addiction to buying expensive toys is his way of getting others to notice him.

Whatever your addiction, you are confusing the pleasure that you feel from doing it as being happiness. When was the last time you looked at yourself in the mirror when you were drunk or using? If you haven't, perhaps you should. I don't think you are going to see a very happy person.

Having been a therapist for several years, I can tell you that I already know why my clients want to see me before they even call to make an appointment. They are unhappy. I have never had anyone call me up and tell me that they wanted to make an appointment with me because they were so damn happy that they couldn't stand it.

What Keeps People from Getting Clean & Sober?

This is an easy answer: Fear. They know what to expect if they continue to drink or use. What they don't know is what will happen if the don't. The drug has been relied upon for so long to cope with and deal with life's terms that giving it up and admitting loss of control are frightening. Even when the known results of continued use will bring continued misery and illness, the addict will still go to what he knows best . . . using.

The addiction to a substance is the strongest addiction you can imagine. One of the strongest addictions is that of nicotine addiction. For those of you who have smoked for years and finally overcame the addiction, you know exactly what I'm talking about. But it can be done and is done so often in today's day and age due to society's willingness to see it as a definite health deterrent and a major cause of cancer.

Another major reason that keeps someone from getting clean and sober is the physical pain and anxiety they feel when they try to stop. Withdrawal symptoms, depending upon the drug, can be so severe that they can cause death. People who are on prescription medication as well as other drugs and alcohol can feel so badly that they would rather continue with their addiction than feel bad. At least while taking the drugs, they don't feel sick. What they don't realize is that the physical withdrawals are only temporary and are often gone within three to five days. Some may even require medical detox to help them through the withdrawal symptoms and for their own physical well-being.

A late stage alcoholic will wake up with the shakes or tremors of the hands. This is due to a deprivation of alcohol while they were either passed out or asleep. Give a few drinks to an alcoholic with the shakes and his shakes will soon dissipate because the cells in the body are getting what they want . . . alcohol. The cells are so used to having the alcohol in the system in order to function as they do and when the alcohol is not there, the cells react in such a way as to cause the shaking, cravings, and general physical illness.

The alcoholic/addict has become dependent not only physically for their drug but also psychologically. They have a love affair with their drug of choice. Many an alcoholic/addict has only a few things in their life that are important to them: Drugs/alcohol, Television, Newspapers, and/or a pet. These things don't talk back. Yet another reason that keeps some from getting clean and sober is that they actually believe that their drinking/using is working for them in spite of the consequences.

Getting Started

To begin the process of dealing with your dependence on alcohol or drugs, I want to restate some things that you will need to believe and put into practice before you even begin to stop your addiction. Until you have come to accept the reality of the next 6 steps, you will not be successful in overcoming your addiction with this book.

1.   The only person you can control is yourself. Any and all attempts to control someone else must cease immediately and you will need to self monitor your behavior to insure that you are not attempting to control someone else. Simply ask yourself, 'is what I am about to say or do going to bring me closer to the person I am about to say or behave towards or will it harm our relationship?' Others will be sure to try to control you but you have a choice on how you react to it. And more importantly: Is what I am about to say or do to myself something that will bring me closer to those things I want in life or will it keep me from them?

2.   No one can make you angry or happy. You have a choice on how you will react to whatever others may say or do to you. You are not a victim of other people's behavior or outside circumstances unless you choose to be a victim. If someone calls you a horse's ass, that's merely their opinion. If two or more people call you a horse's ass, you might want to start shopping around for a saddle. Start taking responsibility for your own life for once and quit blaming others for any or all of your unhappiness.

3.   Everything you do is your best attempt, at the time, to bring you closer to the things that will result in your happiness. Those things you choose to do will either be successful or they will bring you unwanted results. Your choices will be to satisfy one or more of your basic needs of survival, love and belonging, power, freedom, and fun.

Your emotions and physical reactions will be your indicator as to how well your choices are working for you.

4. Whenever you perceive an image in the world outside of yourself that does not match the image you have in your "Quality world," you will begin to rely on the tools you have developed over the years to make these two images match. One thing is for sure: The tool of drugs/alcohol is a tool you have been using for years and it hasn't been working. You will need to develop or discover some more effective tools that will bring you happiness.

5. The only two things we can directly control in our lives are our thoughts and our behavior. By controlling these two components, we indirectly control our emotions and our physiology.

6. You have three choices in dealing with any of the conflict you may experience in your life. If one does not work, the other will.

- 1. Change what you want.
- 2. Change how you behave when you don't get what you want.
- 3. Wherever possible, do both # 1 and # 2.

The six concepts above must be firmly understood and believed for the rest of this book to be effective in overcoming your addiction. Read them several times. They are discussed in detail in the previous chapters if you are having difficulty grasping their true meaning.

I often get phone calls, usually from women, who call me because they are at their wit's end. The conversation goes something like this:

"Mr. Rice?"

'Yes, this is Mike.'

"I got your name out of the phone book and I really need your help. My husband, (or boyfriend) is an alcoholic and I can't make him stop. What can I do?"

What do you think I tell her? My response is always the same: 'Nothing.'

Sometimes, the caller gets very upset and says, "Well, aren't you a drug and alcohol therapist?" (They have tried all that they can think of and nothing has worked so now they are calling me out of desperation and think that all I have to do is wave a magic wand and cure the addict in their life).

'Yes, I am.'

"Then tell me what I can do to make him stop."

Who has the problem here? Is it her husband? No. She is the one who called. She is the one with the problem. Her husband didn't call me. She did. If you were to ask her husband if he had an alcohol problem, what do you think he would say? "Hell no, I don't have a problem. SHE does." And he'd be right. She gets to feel frustrated, choose to depress, choose to get angry, not eat, not sleep, experience aches and pains that her doctor has diagnosed as fibromyalgia and will likely put her on addictive narcotic pain pills.

Then I will ask her, 'What are you doing for you?'

"Pardon me? I don't think I understand the question." She is so caught up in his behavior that she isn't even close to looking at her own needs. He is addicted to alcohol and she is addicted to his addiction.

'If you will allow me to speculate, I bet you have not been eating or sleeping well lately. You're a nervous wreck and feel drained. You have aches and pains and don't feel like getting out of bed half the time, am I right?'

"You're absolutely right."

'You have been complaining to your husband about his drinking; you've blamed him for all of your unhappiness; you've been nagging him for years; you've threatened to leave him; you've punished him by not talking to him and cutting him off from any sexual desires. I'd be willing to say that you may have probably even bribed him somehow if he would quit. Is this correct?'

"You nailed everything that I've been doing."

'Did any of those things work?'

"Hell no, those things made him drink MORE!"

'So what have you been doing for YOU?'

"Well, I guess I haven't been doing anything for me except feeling bad. What can I do?"

'Your husband is addicted to alcohol and you are addicted to your husband.'

This is where I suggest that she go to Al-Anon. Most people are not aware of what Al-Anon is so I explain to them that it is a support group for people like themselves who are married to or have someone in their life that has an alcohol or drug problem. You can find lots of information about Al-Anon when you locate them with Google.

Now, I can't say to this woman, change what you want. To say that would imply that she would want her husband to drink rather than stop drinking. So in this particular case, this conflict resolution would not be effective. She would have to use rule # 2 and change how she reacts when she doesn't get what she wants.

If she quits complaining and nagging her husband about his drinking, do you think he will notice? You bet he will. If she goes out one or two nights a week instead of staying in bed all day and night, do you think he will notice? Absolutely. His conversation might go something like this:

"How come you aren't bitchin' about my drinkin' anymore?"

"Because I'm tired of bitching. It hasn't done a bit of good and has only made things worse and made me feel worse. If you want to drink yourself to death, you go right ahead. I'm just not going to let you take me down with you."

"So where have you been going those nights that you go out? You seein' someone else?"

"You might say that. I've been seeing lots of people. I've been going to an Al-Anon meeting."

"What the hell is Al-Anon?"

"It's a support group for people like me who live with an alcoholic or addict. They got tired of climbing the walls because someone else in their life was addicted to a drug. At least there, I see that I'm not alone and I have a lot of support and help from others."

Now he just *might* say:

"Well maybe I should go to one of those meetings with you just to see what's going on."

"Fine. There's a meeting tonight. I'll get my coat."

But what if he says, "Screw your Al-Anon bullshit!" and he continues to drink and nothing changes? Now she has another choice to make but at least this time, her decision will be much clearer and easier to make. She can decide to either stay in the madness or leave and find her own happiness. She has two choices: 1) Change what she wants, or 2) Change how she reacts when she doesn't get what she wants.

How does choice #1, change what you want, work? If you want world peace, you will eventually become very frustrated because some country will want to control another country and there will always be a war going on somewhere. So quit wanting that. There will be no world peace until the world first learns Choice Theory and puts it into practice. Obviously, choice #1 would mean that she would want him to drink so in this case, choice #1 won't work.

Here's how Choice #2 comes into play: Back in the late 1980's I always wanted a Mercedes SL500, red with palomino interior and both the hard and soft tops. Back then there was no way that I could have afforded the maintenance on such a car much less the car itself. So I could have moped around, felt sorry for myself, chosen to depress over it or . . . is there another car that I like on the market? Sure. The new Mustangs. Does it come in red? Yes. Can you get a convertible? Yes. Is it affordable? Yes. So by changing what I want, the Mustang over the Mercedes, I was satisfied.

How would choice #2, change how you react when you don't get what you want, work? By changing how we react when others behave in ways we find disapproving, we create less stress for ourselves, choose behaviors that are meant only to control ourselves that will create our own happiness and in so doing, will have the effect of causing the other person in your life to change some of their behaviors as well. When you stop using external control, others have a tendency to let up on their use of it as well.

The Real World Versus Your Quality World

Is what you have been doing getting you the results you want in your life?

Many of you will emphatically respond, "YES!" But the reality of the situation is that it is not. Are you happy? Most likely you only feel happy only if and when you are drinking/using. Don't confuse that with happiness. At best, it is only pleasure . . . and temporary as well. You have to continue to drink or use to maintain what you believe to be happiness. That is merely the effect that the drug has on your brain . . . fooling you into believing you are happy. The proof of this can be found when you try to stop. How many times in the past have you tried to quit? Were you initially happy when you were not using/drinking?

What do other people say about your use of drugs or alcohol? Have you lost family and/or friends? Have you lost jobs or dropped out of school? Have you lost a spouse? Do you have any legal problems from drinking/using? Do you have any health problems from drinking/using? Do you have any money problems from drinking/using?

If your life were where you would like it to be, how would it be different than it currently is?

Does your use of drugs or alcohol play any part in keeping you from having those things in life that you would like to have? Were there previous times in your life when you were happier? What were you doing back then that you are not doing today? Take the time to write out exactly how you would like your life to be different than it is today. Once you have done this, look at each area that you would like to have and ask yourself, 'has my alcohol or drug use had anything to do with why I don't have this in my life right now?'

If you are like most addicts/alcoholics, what you want more than anything is to be happy in your relationships with the important people in your life. You also want to have happy relationships and be able to continue drinking or using. One will defeat the other.

Are you willing to do whatever is necessary to get your life where you would like it to be?

If you think that willpower, alone, will get you clean and sober, you will not be successful. While there are those who may overcome their addiction with willpower, the majority of individuals will not and those that do will not have recovered. They would only be what we refer to as dry drunks.

Willpower does play a certain part in overcoming your addiction, but it is much more than that. Your desire for sobriety must be stronger, or at least just as strong, than your desire to drink/use. This may fluctuate once you get started. You must be willing to pay the price of going through some emotional and physical times by controlling your behavior and your thoughts. I'll be the first to tell you that it won't be easy but it may not be as bad as you may think, either. It also would not surprise me that you may relapse once or twice before you finally come to terms with it.

Let's take a look inside your quality world. If you recall from a previous chapter on the quality world, it contains images of those things that are important to you as well as those things that you want that will bring you happiness.

Right now, your drinking or drug of choice is in your quality world and all of the things that used to be important to you are only vague images in your quality world. You, and only you, can take the image of alcohol or drugs out of your quality world. Usually, this is done by replacing it with something else. Some people replace it with A.A.., some replace it with their faith, others have been known to replace it with what may be considered by some as a positive addiction e.g. working out, drinking gallons of tea, reading, working or staying busy, developing a hobby, etc. If, however, whatever you replace it with causes significant problems in other areas of your life, then it is not a positive addiction. You would be merely trading one addiction for another. You will need to replace it with something else that will give you happiness and better relationships.

Your years of use of alcohol or drugs have fooled your quality world into believing that they bring you happiness when, actually, they are only giving you short-lived pleasure. That's why you have to keep using them in order to maintain it. True, pleasure may be more intense than happiness but happiness is the longer lasting of the two. And the key to happiness? -- having meaningful relationships with the important people in our lives.

When it comes to love and belonging, if you have alcohol or drugs in your quality world, I have seen the drugs or the alcohol win over love and belonging with the addict most every time. This is not to say that given the choice of one or the other, one will always choose their drug of choice. There have been addicts/alcoholics who have quit when their only option was to quit or lose their significant other and/or family. Generally speaking though, the drug will win most of the time.

I would like to make a recommendation at this time for you to replace your present addiction with something that is much better than what you presently have: Happiness. But right now, you will have to take my word for it. You aren't going to find it right at this moment or just because you just stopped drinking or using. You will, however, begin to notice others may start to lighten up on you with their complaining, criticizing, threatening, etc. This change will bring you some happiness, I'm sure, but probably not as much as you would currently like to have, but it will be more than you've had for awhile. Trust me. It gets better. You will start to recognize opportunities and perceive things with a different attitude. And along with this you will begin to feel energized and motivated to climb out of your funk and once again take control of your life.

Which would you rather have, happiness or an addiction; happiness or hangovers; happiness or loss of friends, family, and/or spouse; happiness or shame and guilt; happiness or loss of job; happiness or legal problems; happiness or health problems; happiness or loss of home or children? If you choose happiness, then you have chosen something far greater than the alcohol or drug that you presently have in your quality world. You won't be able to maintain both for very long. If you prefer happiness, how does drinking or using drugs help you acquire the happiness that you want?

I know what you're thinking. "If I cut down or cut back on my drug or alcohol use, I'll get a little bit of happiness instead of a lot of happiness. And some happiness is better than no happiness." Sorry. It doesn't work that way. Cutting down or cutting back always leads to using more in the long run. Remember, addictions are progressive. Cutting back on your drinking or drug use is like a woman saying, "I'm just a little bit pregnant."

One of the major problems we alcoholics/addicts have is that we want what we want, NOW. You have been drinking or using for a number of years and turning things around will not happen instantly. It will take some time just as it took some time for you to get addicted. Plus, you will need to learn some new ways of dealing with life on life's terms rather than your terms. But once you learn them, they will become your terms.

After several thousand years of addiction in this world, we have a pretty good idea of what works and what doesn't work. You've been doing things your way and I would presume that it hasn't worked so far. Otherwise, you wouldn't be reading this book.

Just recently, I had a group member who has a history of legal problems, marriage problems, and job problems focus on a part of life that is causing him to totally miss the point. Missing the point is what keeps addicts and alcoholics addicted. He received a DUI because of THC metabolites from cannabis in his blood and has lost his license for a year. He compares marijuana to alcohol and sees pot as less of a drug than alcohol.

In an effort to make my point, I said to him, 'why don't you rob banks, then?' And he replied, "cause robbing banks are against the law." I responded, 'and marijuana is not against the law to use?'

My client went into an uproar about me comparing apples to oranges and that one can not make a good analogy using the comparison of bank robbery to smoking pot. The point is: <u>They are both against the law</u>.

Failing to see this point, he continues to argue the comparison of bank robbery to pot use as being an unfair comparison. He just doesn't get it . . . yet. It is just this sort of short sighted thinking that has caused his life to be so unproductive and cluttered with unhappiness.

This book is not the only way one can overcome addictions. As a reminder, there are other programs that have a track record of success. Probably the most successful to date has been Alcoholics Anonymous. This 73 year old program is still going strong and there is not another self-sustaining program that can make this claim. There are also programs such as Rational Recovery, Salvation Army, Veteran's Association, various religious programs. You'll find several certified alcohol and drug treatment agencies who have worked with thousands of people just like yourself and know what it takes to get you through it.

Another stumbling block many an addict/alcoholic has is the thought that, "I'm not your typical alcoholic (or addict). You don't know what I've gone through. All of this stuff that is supposed to help get someone sober or clean may work for some people but it won't work for me. I'm different than all those other addicts or alcoholics. If you had gone through what I've experienced in life, you'd be an alcoholic or addict too." To this I would like to say, 'horse hockey!'

You are no different than any other alcoholic or addict. You are addicted to a substance that controls you rather then the other way around. Whatever has happened to you in the past has nothing to do with why you are an alcoholic or addict. It may be why you began drinking or using but it is not why you are addicted. You and every other addict/alcoholic possess a lot of shame and guilt so you all have this in common.

For whatever happened to you in the past, I am truly sorry. But that is what it is, the past. Nothing anyone can say or do can change that fact that whatever happened, happened. As long as you choose to stay in the past, you are choosing to remain a victim of someone else's behavior and since we can only control our own behavior, why relinquish your control to someone else?

I have clients who come to see me for issues other than drugs or alcohol. Many times, they seem to get a little upset if I don't ask them about their past. They seem to want to blame their behavior problems and unhappiness on something that happened a long time ago. There are many therapists who are very willing to go back into the past. It has been my experience that when a therapist does this, the client leaves the therapist's office feeling worse than he or she did when they first walked into the office. Why open up old wounds. Why pick off scabs that cause one to bleed? I don't want you feeling worse when you leave my office than you did when you came in.

It isn't important at all what happened to you in the past. Did it have a direct effect on you? Absolutely. Can you change whatever it was that happened to you? Absolutely not. How would you rather feel: happy or sad and miserable? If you said, "happy," then let's talk about what you can do to find happiness instead of feeling bad about something you can't change. We can't change the past but we can certainly change the NOW and TOMORROW. To continue to ruminate about any injustices you may have incurred in the past will do no more than to keep you stuck in the role of a victim. Seeing yourself as a victim will give you an excuse for not taking responsibility for finding your own happiness and success in life.

Like many of you, I have experienced a lot of unhappiness and injustices in my life. And, like many of you, I continued to see myself as a victim and would drink to deal with all of the unhappiness and unwanted emotions I would have whenever I thought about my past. So get up off of your pity pot, stop feeling sorry for yourself, and start to take responsibility for your happiness. Doing so will give you a sense of self-respect and right now, that will probably be the only respect anyone is willing to give you at this time. But don't worry. Once you begin to take responsibility, others will begin to respect you too. No one else can make you happy. Happiness is an "inside job." Happiness is the result of your decision to be happy and to avoid all negative emotions and thoughts that will destroy happiness. Since you can only directly control your thoughts and your acting, you have two choices that will result in less stress, less anger, and lead you to happiness and peace of mind: 1. Change what you want. 2. Change how you react when you don't get what you want. And whenever possible, do both #1 and #2.

I'm glad I experienced all of the hardship, hurts, wounds, injustices, heartaches, and horrible experiences in my life. These are the things that make up who and what I am. From these experiences I have learned to be thankful, humble, and grateful. They have been life's lessons that had a positive result because I chose to see them in a positive way rather than the negative way that I had been doing for years. My life didn't change until I changed how I perceived my past. I would not be a therapist or writing this book if those things had not occurred in my life. To quote Dr. Robert H. Schuller, "Turn your scars into stars and your hurts into haloes."

So here is what you should have discovered about yourself so far:

You are unhappy, so admit it.

You have been dealing with your unhappiness by using drugs or alcohol. So admit that too.

People in your quality world have not been behaving the way you want them to behave so you've been trying to control them with the seven deadly habits (and they've been using them on you). Admit it.

You drink or use because you think *others* pissed you off instead of seeing that you are choosing to be pissed off. Admit it.

You also drink because you like how it makes you feel as long as you are drinking   Admit it.

Your uses of drugs/alcohol have not given you the true happiness you want in life. In fact, they are the cause for most, if not all, of you unhappiness. Admit it.

You want the important people in your life to respect you. Admit it.

You have lost control of your drug or alcohol use. Admit it.

Just look at all of the things that exist in your real world and how they fail to even come close to those things that you want in your quality world.   No wonder you're unhappy. What if I told you that all you had to do was just one thing and all of those things would begin to change? Would you do it or would you rather continue feeling miserable like you do?

What is that one thing that you might try to do that you haven't been doing so far? Duh. If what you have been doing all along has not been working, why keep doing it? If what you have been doing all along has been making your life's situation worse, why keep doing it? If you're tired of getting emotionally beat up each and every day, did it ever occur to you to not get into the ring?

Here's why you have been continuing to use or drink:

You don't know how you will cope with your day to day stress if you stop.

Even though you may not like your drinking or using, at least you know what to expect if you keep it up. You don't know what to expect if you quit.

You don't like how you feel when you stop. You have all sorts of withdrawal symptoms with irritability and feeling sick heading the list. And you would rather drink/use than feel sick and miserable even though it causes you other problems.

You have always been able to depend on the effects of drugs or alcohol and that's why you have been using them. If you quit, you don't know what you can depend on to deal with the stress you feel (your unhappiness) most of the time.

Another major reason some people fail to stop their addiction is due to their shame and guilt. Alcohol and drugs work wonders for making those unwanted thoughts and emotions go away.

Guilt is: "I did something wrong."

Shame is: "I AM something wrong."

Put these two thoughts together and you have an emotional and physical reaction that is equivalent to 10 pounds of turkey crap in a 5 pound bag.

And finally . . . "I tried quitting before and it doesn't work." It didn't work because you didn't do all the things you were supposed to do in order to quit. You either didn't try or you only tried half-heartedly. To say a specific drug/alcohol program doesn't work is like taking a new TV back to where you bought it and telling them that it doesn't work. "Did you get a picture?"

"No."

"Did you get any sound?"

"No,"

"Did you plug it in?"

"No. It doesn't work."

I can't make you or anyone else stop drinking or using. I don't have that kind of power. But what I can do is show you some possible tools other than drinking or drugs that you might want to try and see if they make your life happier. What have you got to lose? You have everything to gain.

116

Based upon what you have read so far, do you have a problem with alcohol or drugs, or not? If not, put the book down and just keep on keepin' on the way you have been for the last several years. If you stay on the same path you have been on, where do you see yourself in the next couple of years? On the other hand, if you admit you have a problem, let's continue.

OK. So you have come to the actual realization that you have an alcohol or drug problem and that you need to do something about it. Right?

Assignment One

You mean I gotta do homelearning? Did you think that all you had to do was read a book and you'd be cured of all of your demons?

What is it that you want? Say it out loud. Now write it out on a piece of paper. It should say:

"I want to be clean and sober for the rest of my life."

"I want to be happy for the rest of my life."

"I want meaningful relationships for the rest of my life."

How important is it to you to want to be clean and sober?

If you merely want it without that true burning or desire, you only have a wish, at best, which is not intense enough to get you what you want.

Are you willing to do whatever it takes to get to be clean and sober?

If not, go back and read some more from the beginning of this book. You just may not be ready yet.

I tried to stop smoking at least 20 times over the years before I actually succeeded. I would always relapse after one or two weeks. I could never really do what I had to do to quit until I saw a real need to have to quit. What did it for me? I saw the statistics of how many people die each year due to smoking cigarettes. I was tired of getting bronchitis twice a year. The cost of cigarettes was getting ridiculous at over $4.50 per pack which, for a two pack a day smoker came to $3,240.00 a year and all I had to show for it was poor health and a hacking cough.

I also had to employ the principles of A.A. and the help of God to quit. I kept telling myself, if God were to walk up to me today, what would he say to me if He saw me pull out a cigarette and light it up? He would probably tell me how I was destroying the gift that He had given me by putting things in me that would harm or destroy me. Would He be happy to see me smoking? I would venture to say, 'No.' As well as utilizing those two methods to give up my smoking habit, I also had one other very important element that made it successful. I had to really want to quit this time. The other times had been no more than just wishes.

None of us will change anything in our lives unless we see a need to do so. The first few days, I saw the need to quit. But after awhile, I no longer saw the need so I would relapse. Unless we can see the need to quit on a day to day basis, nothing will change. Once it does change, rarely do we need to focus on the need on a daily basis.

What kept me from quitting in the past? My fear of how I would get along in life without a cigarette. I feared how irritable, jittery, and how physically bad I felt when I stopped smoking in the past. I had been smoking for 43 years and could not visualize myself without a cigarette in my hand. I had to change some images in my quality world.

Instead of visualizing on all of the negatives, I began to see the positives. I began to see myself with pink and healthy lungs with no more wheezing, huffing, and puffing especially after intimate moments. I began to see myself healthy instead of lying in a casket -- all because I wanted to look cool when I was smoking. I followed the instructions on the Patch instead of racing through the time period that they are supposed to be used. This helped get me through the physical withdrawals.

I had tried the patch before but I never followed the instructions (typical addict). I wanted relief NOW. To hell with following the instructions. Every time I used the patch before, I felt good without smoking and would advance to the next lower level of nicotine patch before I was instructed to do so. Consequently, I would relapse each and every time. If you use the patch, RTFM. (Read the friggin' manual).

<u>You have to want sobriety or to be clean, and you have to be willing to do those things that will cause it to happen.</u> If you don't see a need to get better, you won't. It doesn't have to hurt to give up your drug of choice. If you are having physical withdrawals, there are medically supervised programs to get you past that stage so that you don't have to suffer like you have in the past when you tried to quit on your own. If you need help . . . ASK. Get what you need from others! It's not a sign of weakness. To not get help is the opposite of being smart.

Don't be so anxious to get through all the assignments. It took you a long time to become addicted and it will take a long time to overcome your addiction. Take it slow and deliberate. Work your 1st assignment at least for 2 or more days before moving on to the next assignment. So spend the next two days thinking about and visualizing how nice it would be to be rid of a drug or alcohol that is controlling you instead of you controlling it. You will look better. You will feel better. People will begin to like you and you will have friends that you enjoy. You will be happier. You will sleep better.

The camel is often associated with A.A. He begins and ends each day on his knees and he can go all day without a drink. Emulate the camel. Don't look any further than today. There's no day, but today and today you are not going to drink or use. Tomorrow is another day and treat it the same as this day.

What do you think the important people in your life will do when you have gotten clean and sober? How will they react to you if you are not drugged by alcohol or other drugs? Will they be more receptive to you or would they be repelled by your sobriety? Will they like you better sober or intoxicated?

Do you want to live the rest of your life as miserable or worse than you have for these last several years? Can you see how you are the one that put yourself in this position and how you can also be the person who can take you out of it? Only this time, you have help from others to do it so you won't be alone.

Assignment Two

Over the years, you have been attempting to get one or more of your basic needs met by the use of alcohol and/or drugs. Do you recall the five basic needs? They are:

- Survival
- Love & Belonging
- Power & self worth
- Freedom
- Fun

Using the scale described by Glasser, (1995) on a scale of one to 5, with 5 being the highest score, how important to you are each of these basic needs? Circle each one as to the degree of importance you place on them.

	1	2	3	4	5
Survival					
Love & Belonging					
Power					
Freedom					
Fun					

Now that you see what is important to you, these are the things that you need in your life to make you happy.

Using an "X", mark from one to five the number you feel that you currently possess in your life. Any "X" that is two or more numbers away from your circled number is that part of your life that is missing, the core of your unhappiness, and the focus of why you have been using drugs or alcohol to fill that void in your life.

If the gap is in the need for survival, perhaps you have lost your job or several jobs due to your use and now you have trouble not only buying your alcohol or drug, but you may be on the verge of homelessness, begging for food, etc. You most likely will also be low in the area of power and self-worth if Survival is affected. If you are low in possession of Survival needs, you are deep within your addiction and need professional help.

If the gap is in the need for Love, as most alcoholics/addicts are, you have lost the important people in your life: A spouse, a mother or father, a sibling, or perhaps your children.

If you have conflict with a boss, a teacher, or a co-worker, you are low in the area of power and self-worth. Self Worth is also affected sometimes in divorces and being fired. Most alcoholics and addicts feel powerless in their life. Loss of friends also affects self-worth, loss of respect, love and belonging.

Several incarcerations for DUIs, public intoxication, drug possession and paraphernalia charges are all a part of loss of freedom due to incarceration. Low survival possession also contributes to not being able to have the freedom to come and go and do the things that you need to do to help rise above your shortcomings.

Lonely and bored individuals will have low possession scores of Fun and Love. This need is often a major reason why alcohol or drugs are used. When asked why people drink or do drugs, the majority of them will say, "To have fun." What they are really saying is, "I'm bored, lonely, and don't have any love in my life." They use alcohol and drugs to compensate for what they don't have. The thought may be, "a few drinks caused me to feel happy. Maybe a lot of drinks will make me really happy." The problem with that is, only a few drinks work like that effectively. Going overboard with drinks only causes depression and unhappiness.

OK. Let's evaluate some more. If you continue to drink or use drugs:

Will your survival needs improve? Will you acquire gainful employment? Have adequate income? Be able to afford housing, food, clothing, and transportation? How much are you spending on your drug of choice or alcohol on a weekly basis? If you continue to drink and/or use drugs, where do you think you will be in one or more years?

If you continue to drink and/or use drugs, will you find love and belonging or will you have even less than you have now?

If you continue to drink and/or use drugs, will it allow you take back control of your life or will the drug or the alcohol have control over you?

If you continue to drink or use drugs, how much freedom can you expect to have?

If you continue to drink or use drugs, tell me how much fun you've been having lately.

By now it should be clear to you that what you have been doing to attempt to get your basic needs met has done nothing but cause you to be distanced from them instead of bringing them closer to you. However, if you don't see this, then just keep on doing what you've been doing since it seems to be doing so well for you.

So many people who are addicted will rationalize and say, "Well, at least I'm not dead, so I must not have a problem." They see death as the only way out or near death as the time they may start to do something about their addiction after most of the harm has been done. Addicts and alcoholics are afraid to live and afraid to die. As Fr. Martin says, on his DVD *Chalk Talk, Revised.* "They're just, afraid." (1976).

What You Can Expect When You Quit

Depending on what you have been using and how long you have been doing it will play a part in what you may or may not experience. If you are fortunate, your withdrawal symptoms may not be all that noticeable to you other than feeling "out of sorts," or having cravings for the substance. You can expect unhappiness at the start. Your body will need to adjust to not getting the drug or the alcohol that you've been putting into it on a somewhat regular basis.

With Marijuana, you can expect:

- irritability
- anxiety
- physical tension
- decreases in appetite and mood
- poor sleep

Symptoms of marijuana withdrawal first appear within 24 hours. Withdrawal is most pronounced for the first 10 days and can last up to 28 days.

Methamphetamine withdrawal symptoms include but are not limited to:

- fatigue
- long, disturbed periods of sleep
- irritability
- intense hunger
- moderate to severe depression
- psychotic reactions such as seeing or hearing things, paranoia, psychosis
- anxiety
- poor sleep
- using dreams

Meth withdrawal, length and severity of depression is related to how much and how often Meth was used. Withdrawal symptoms including, cravings, exhaustion, depression, mental confusion, restlessness, insomnia, deep or disturbed sleep, may last up to 48 hours. You may have nightmares or even dreams of using. These will ease up the longer you remain clean and sober.

Alcohol Withdrawal symptoms

Mild symptoms of alcohol withdrawal include

* irritability
* anxiety
* fatigue
* mild cravings for alcohol
* insomnia

People may feel slightly shaky, or have cold and clammy hands. Alcohol withdrawal can also affect appetite, making it difficult to eat. Both nausea and vomiting are common alcohol withdrawal symptoms. Diarrhea may also be a concern.

More significant symptoms of alcohol withdrawal suggest the possibility of experiencing the DTs. People may have dilated pupils, involuntary movements, and tremors. These symptoms suggest that alcohol withdrawal should take place at a treatment facility or hospital, where symptoms can be addressed, and medical emergencies can be handled.

The DTs can create confusion and disturbing visual hallucinations. People may also experience heart arrhythmias or palpitations, high fever, and convulsions. A medical facility can stop many of these symptoms by giving low dose anti-convulsions or barbiturates during the first few days of alcohol withdrawal.

It is tremendously important that people with a long history of alcohol use withdraw under medical care. Irregular heart rhythms and convulsions can cause death if not addressed. Untreated DTs can cause death in up to 20% of people undergoing alcohol withdrawal.

Physical symptoms of alcohol withdrawal tend to occur about 12 hours after a person's last drink, and will peak within two to three days. Insomnia, mood instability and fatigue may linger for several months after one has detoxed.

Maintaining sobriety is further helped by regular attendance at support groups for alcoholics like Alcoholics Anonymous. Some find that voluntary hospitalization at a treatment center is beneficial in maintaining sobriety during the first months.

Heroin and other opiates

With regular heroin use, tolerance develops. This means the abuser must use more heroin to achieve the same intensity of effect. As higher doses are used over time, physical dependence and addiction develop. With physical dependence, the body has adapted to the presence of the drug and withdrawal symptoms may occur if use is reduced or stopped.

Withdrawal, which in regular abusers may occur as early as a few hours after the last administration, produces

- drug craving
- restlessness

- muscle and bone pain
- insomnia
- diarrhea and vomiting
- cold flashes with goose bumps ("cold turkey")
- kicking movements ("kicking the habit")
- and other symptoms.

Major withdrawal symptoms peak between 48 and 72 hours after the last dose and subside after about a week. Sudden withdrawal by heavily dependent users who are in poor health is occasionally fatal, although heroin withdrawal is considered less dangerous than alcohol or barbiturate withdrawal.

Emotional Overload

You can also expect a floodgate of emotions to enter your life when you quit drinking or using. You have been avoiding most if not all of your unwanted emotions through the use of alcohol or drugs. Once you cease using or drinking, years of emotions will begin to surface. You will have days where seemingly, you emotionally feel like you've been run over by a Mack truck. These unwanted emotions may come on with little to no warning. There is only one way to deal with them in a healthy manner . . . First identify the emotion. Is it fear, anger, frustration, or what?

Once you have identified the emotion, what, or who seems to be in front of this emotion? Who do you associate the emotion with? Your spouse? Your siblings? Your ex spouse? Yourself? Whomever it is, know right here and now that you have a choice of going with this unwanted emotion and feeling bad or you can choose to turn this emotion around and feel either neutral or good. Your emotion about this person is an emotion that you have chosen to have about this person. You could, just as easily, choose not to have an emotion about this person. Ask someone what the opposite of Love is and most people will respond, "hate." Not so. The opposite of love is indifference . . . where you don't care one way or the other about the other person. If it were hate, you would still have an emotional tie to that person based upon your choice to have negative feelings about that person.

Whatever the situation may be, understand that it is something that is going on only in your own mind at this time and place. If it is someone else, they aren't even around so you are creating this emotion yourself. If it is yourself that you are upset with, then you will need to deal with the things about yourself that need to change. The time has come for you to stop blaming others for your unhappiness and begin taking responsibility for your own happiness.

Self-evaluation is paramount to finding all of the happiness and peace of mind that you have been needing and wanting for perhaps several years. You will also need to work on your Shame and Guilt which we will cover later.

The above are all of the negative things to expect. You will also experience some positive results and the longer you stay with it, the more you will receive such as:

- More money in your pocket.
- More restful sleep (after your body has detoxed and adjusted)
- People will begin to treat you in ways that you have wanted them to do for a long time. It may take a little longer for those whom you have harmed the most to come around but they will.

Your sustained abstinence will be the proof they need before they begin to believe you.

- You will be much happier.
- You will feel much better with increased vigor, stamina, and no hangovers.
- You'll remember all that you say and do.
- You will begin to see things much more clearly and be able to express yourself better.
- You will be more productive at work.
- You will have healthier friends and learn how to have fun without drugs/alcohol.
- You will like yourself much better.
- You will discover that happiness lasts a long time but pleasure is short-lived.
- You will realize that long term periods of happiness are far better than split second pleasures.
- You will begin eating better and more healthfully.
- You will have meaningful relationships with those with whom you want to have meaningful relationships.
- You will find yourself genuinely loving yourself and others, and others loving you.
- You will have found TOTAL HAPPINESS.

But none of this will occur overnight.

For Someone Who Loves or Lives With an Addict/Alcoholic.

With what other alcoholic or drug addict on this planet would you be willing to leave you kids?

Buckle your seatbelt for a wilder ride than Mr. Toad ever had. Your loved one is going through some emotional, psychological, and even spiritual changes by making an attempt to give up his/her drug or choice. Just be there and support them in their suffering. There's nothing you can do for them except offer positive support.

They are going to hurt and you don't want them to. They are going to be emotional, and you will think it's all about you. They are going to be angry and it will appear they are taking it out on you . . . and they are because you just happen to be the closest person there. Don't take it personally even though it will be directed at you. Sometimes, all you need to do is give them a hug. And sometimes, they will not want you even to get close to them, much less hug them.

Just keep letting them know that what they are going through is only temporary and will soon be over and that they have a whole lifetime of health and happiness ahead of them. Get your butt to an Al-Anon meeting. Suggest your loved one go to an A.A. meeting and go with them if it will help them to go. Whatever you do, don't use any of the seven deadly habits. (Criticizing, Blaming, Complaining, Nagging, Threatening, Punishing, Bribing/Rewarding). Above all, don't give them any money for drugs or alcohol to ease their suffering. Don't purchase any drugs or alcohol yourself for them. Don't provide transportation to any locations where they can score their drug of choice.

When your significant other stops drinking or using, several things are going to happen with both of you. Much of the behavior exhibited when under the influence will begin to disappear. But many on the behaviors you have been using over the last several months or years will be the same and will consist of many of the seven deadly habits as well as a lot of hurts and anger from the past. Recovery is a minimum two party program and if there is a family involved, recovery is a family program. It's not so surprising that many marriages end in divorce after the other party stops using or drinking.

He is used to seeing you and others while influenced by years of drug or alcohol use. Now that he is not using/drinking, he will see you and others in a different light with different attitudes. You, however, will still be used to nagging, complaining, etc and saying and doing things out of habit that won't be necessary to do anymore. You will still feel angry and wounded about all of the past behaviors said and done when he was drinking and using. For this reason, either continue with Al-Anon or get professional counseling. You may even be a stranger to him if he had been drinking or using before he met you now that he's clean and sober. There are many things that must be worked out together along with your significant other's   being   abstinent.

All My Friends

Right now, your best friend is your favorite drink or drug. It has been there for you during your darkest days, soothing your emotional pain and filling a void of loneliness and despair. All you had to do was look up this friend and you would begin to feel better right away.

But did it ever occur to you that this friend may be why you are feeling so lonely, miserable, and without anyone else to understand what you are feeling or perceiving what you are going through?

Has your drinking or drugging brought you closer to your happiness and goals or has it driven them away?

Has your drinking or drugging brought you successful people in your life or has it introduced you to people no better off or worse than you are at this time in your life?

What do you think successful and happy people think about the use of drugs and alcohol in their own lives?

Did it ever occur to you that perhaps the reason why you are so unhappy is because your drinking or drugging has caused all of the important people in your life to go away?

This may be a bit difficult for you at this time and you may not want to hear it but it is an important part of your success in getting clean and sober. For perhaps the last several years, the only friends you may have are those who share your drug/alcohol interests. Everyone else has been criticizing you, nagging you, complaining, threatening you, punishing you, or even bribing you to get you to stop your substance use. Your current friends who drink or use drugs don't do that. In fact, they seem to be the only ones who understand you and your needs right now.

Sorry to tell you this, but they only want your company to commiserate in their own unhappiness. Addicts and alcoholics hate to drink or use alone if they don't have to. They'll even do their best to get you to drink or use with them even though you've told them that you have quit and that you're going to be clean and sober. Eventually they will begin to drink alone because they have detached from others and don't want anyone to see them in their drunken state and disarray.

Alcoholics and addicts attach to those things that don't talk back: such as television, newspapers, pets, video games. Female alcoholics are usually all alone with the exception of a bird, or a cat, or both. I don't know if you've ever noticed this in others or even perhaps yourself, but have you ever seen what long term drinking or drug use does to your physical appearance? It really shows itself in women, it seems more than men. It ages you tremendously. Before and after photos of drinkers and addicts are incredible to see. They appear to be no more than an empty shell of a person when drinking or using. Once people get clean and sober, there is a gleam in the eye indicating spirit, a happy life, and physical wellbeing. The face no longer is swollen or puffy in the drinker or drawn and taut in the user.

Moving away from the people you have in your life right now may be scary because they may be the only friends you have. Avoiding them would mean you would not have any friends. But this is not necessarily true. You may have family and other non-using friends that may have distanced themselves from you due to your past use. If you find yourself without friends when you quit, then go to several

A.A. meetings.   You will meet accepting friends right away.

Marilyn, whom I spoke about earlier, had this to say about her experience with Al-Anon after she finally went.

"Go. Don't think about it. Go. You kept on coaxing me to go – you kept on me until I actually did it. I got so much from Al-Anon so soon because I had been trying to solve my own problem for so long – using the control factor on myself – I didn't want to admit that I was powerless – I saw and heard from others who were able to admit their powerlessness over their situation and admit it and feel better because they admitted it. I had heard similar advice from family and friends, but for some reason it meant even more to hear from complete strangers who were hurting because of the addiction of a loved one. I was not alone in loving an addict and facing the pain of being unable to "fix it."   The "Anon" was key for me --- an inviting social context where you could say anything and people would not judge or betray you inner most thoughts.   Strangers were crying and laughing together because they share a similar sad situation with an addicted loved one.   Go. Don't think about going. Go."

Our addictions are all centered on our relationships, or lack of them. For those of you who utilize A.A. you will find many people who are willing to be your friend. That's why it's called the Fellowship.   Reconnect with family and friends of the past. The Big Book of A.A. and the 12 steps will help show you how to do this.

Right now you need to hang out with people who are non-judgmental; people who have been where you are AND people who have *never* been where you are. Their words, behaviors, advice, attitudes, etc. are just what you need to learn to remain free from the clutches of your addiction. You will find people like this in treatment programs, A.A., and other fellowship programs.

Substance dependence keeps you from receiving important information about how to deal and live in the world. It smothers your emotional, physical, and spiritual receivers so that none of those things ever get past your filters and into your quality world and tool box. Your perceptions are vague, blurry, and far from being correct. Once you get sober and begin recovery, you will begin to see the world and other people much clearer than before. You will see things differently and things will begin to take on new and exciting meanings. Until then, you won't see the Real World, you only see a Fantasy World.

How Important Is Friendship?

Friendship is paramount in helping you overcome your addiction. If you are a heavy drinker or user, you probably don't seem to want any satisfying relationships. In the words of the late Joe E. Lewis, who died from alcoholism, "a friend in need is a pest." Mr. Lewis was not a happy man.

The major cause of most unhappiness is the result of not having satisfying relationships. Satisfying relationships will be at the core of all happiness and good mental health.

Because we are all hard-wired for social contact, we need to feel connected, accepted, loved, and have a sense of belonging. If you want to know the key to happiness, you will find it in your ability to have and maintain long term, non-obligatory relationships with others . . . especially with those with whom you want to have a meaningful relationship. The minimum number you will need is one. However, the more you have the more happiness you will experience.

Those who lack happiness are those who do not have healthy and satisfying relationships. They may have a history of failed or unhappy relationships so they have detached from others to avoid any further unhappy relationships. This is a major reason why they drink or use drugs. Those who lack happiness have detached from others, isolate, or *disappear*. Alcohol and drugs are the most common and most effective way to disappear, with the exception of suicide.

Many of us in Choice Theory contend that most of what is being called "mental illness" is no more than unhappy people . . . people who are in conflict with other people in their lives with whom they would like to have a better relationship. With the exception of cerebral palsy, mental retardation, Alzheimer's, and Parkinson's disease, the symptoms commonly referred to as mental illness in the DSM IV are no more than behaviors of unhappy people with unsatisfying relationships. They have tried all that they know to do and have used every tool in their tool kit to make their real world match their quality world and nothing has been successful. Instead, some may isolate or detach, others may crawl into bottles of alcohol or use drugs, while many others may become very creative and find other ways to behave to compensate for whatever they feel is missing in their life . . . meaningful relationships. They do this by choosing to depress, behaving in a manner that would be diagnosed as obsessive compulsive disorder, choosing to be anxious, developing so-called schizophrenic behaviors, behaving in a manner that the psychiatric delivery system would label as bi-polar, ADD, or ADHD, or any other so-called mental disorder as found in the Diagnostic and

Statistical Manual of Mental Disorder, Fourth Edition (DSM-IV).

You can not maintain a meaningful and satisfying relationship with anyone for very long if you utilize the seven deadly habits of external control. You can not maintain a meaningful and satisfying relationship with anyone for very long if you use alcohol or drugs. You can not maintain a meaningful and satisfying relationship with anyone for very long if you push others away, distance yourself, or isolate from others. Yet these are the things people do when someone else in their life is behaving in a way in which they disapprove. What is needed is a new tool that resolves conflict without driving you or the other person away. And this tool is called, Choice Theory.

What is meant by "non-obligatory" relationship? A non-obligatory relationship is one is which neither of you feel obligated to the other for any reason other than faithfulness and trust. It means that one person can choose to do one thing and not have to worry about how the other person will behave or react. You accept them for who and what they are even if it is different from you. You would never consider trying to change them or use any of the seven deadly habits on them. If you did, you would be quick to apologize to them. You would never destroy their hopes or dreams and they would not do so to you.

Years ago, I used to wonder, "Why is it that a man and a woman can be the best of friends but the minute they have sex together, BAM! The entire relationship has changed. I now believe that it is the result of feeling obligated to the other person since they got sexually involved. It's almost as if they are saying to one another: "OK. You gave yourself to me (or I gave myself to you) so now we are committed in a relationship." Following this thought is the perception of "ownership" and "obligation." "You're mine and I'm yours. Now you must do what I say." This tacit obligation will now serve to lead the way to external control and use of the seven deadly habits.

As an example, let's say that you approach your close friend and invite him to attend some function that you both enjoy. He may have other needs or priorities and politely turn down your offer. He may say something such as, "Boy I'd love to go but my car hasn't been running too well lately and if I don't get it fixed this weekend, I may not be able to get to work next week. You go ahead and tell me all about it when you get back." To his response you would probably say, "OK. Sorry you couldn't go. I'll see ya' later."

After leaving your friend, you approach your spouse or significant other and invite her to go to this same function. She might say something like: "I'd love to go but I have a hair appointment this afternoon," whereupon you respond immediately with, "Goddamnit! You NEVER do anything with me when I ask you!"

What's the difference between the two scenarios? You behaved in a positive way with your best friend that didn't harm the relationship when he declined the offer yet you behaved in a way that harmed the relationship with your spouse, the person you love. Your friend is a nonobligatory relationship but your spouse is a controlled or obligatory relationship. Is it any wonder why we divorce our spouses more than we divorce our friends?

One of the most common statements I heard growing up in my family, as well as in the rest of the world is, "I didn't want to hurt your feelings." If the only person we can control is ourselves and if another person's feelings become hurt, then who is responsible for those hurt feelings? The person who feels hurt, that's who. They chose to react the way they did. They are choosing to hurt their own feelings. The other person didn't "make them feel that way" anymore than when you did the exercise of visualizing people you don't like vs. people you do like in an earlier chapter. Even if it were possible to hurt your feelings, which feeling of yours did they hurt?

When someone says something to you or does something that you disapprove of, you have two of the most powerful tools in the world that you can use. Instead, you have been using all the wrong tools or even making up some new tools of your own that haven't worked either. So here are those two tools:

1. Change what you want.

You can't feel hurt, or angry, or happy, or sad, or any other positive or negative emotion without thinking something. Whatever your thoughts, you create a subsequent emotion and physical reaction. In simple terms, you can control your own thoughts and you do this by choosing those things you want to think about. If you are not getting what you want, then change what you want.

2. Change how you react when you don't get what you want.

All we do from birth until death is behave and *all behavior is chosen*. Our behavior is our best attempt at the time to do something that will result in meeting one or more of our basic needs that we want that will result in causing happiness. You have a choice of reacting in ways that are not happy, neutral, or happy.

So now I refer you back to the Total Behavior concept of the auto with the two front wheels that are controlled by the driver: Thoughts and Acting. Change what you want; you are controlling your thoughts. Change how you react (acting) when you don't get what you want, you are controlling your behavior. By controlling your thoughts and/or your actions, you are indirectly controlling how you feel both emotionally and physically.

You have conditioned yourself over the years to reach for a bottle or a drug the minute you felt unhappy and had unwanted physical reactions in your body or generally felt physically uncomfortable. The slightest change between your real world perception and your quality world wants has been leading you to use or drink all of the time. Why? . . . because you don't have to wait long for the drug to take effect. You get instant gratification and your brain is tricked into thinking you are happy.

You have the power to start using new methods in controlling your alcohol or drug use. The hard part comes from learning how to use them. There's no easy way to teach you this other than to say, you have to experience some painful and unwanted emotions and reactions and apply them when you are experiencing these painful and unwanted emotions. Again, and I can not stress this enough, this is the absolute acceptance and understanding on your part that you can choose how you will react and behave. It won't be easy at first. In fact, it will be damn difficult and you will be tempted to go back into your old ways of doing things. But keep in mind, if your old ways were effective tools, you wouldn't be reading this book right now.

Drugs and alcohol may work faster to ease your pain but you have to keep doing them in order for them to continue to work. Their effectiveness is only temporary, at best, until they eventually end up taking your life. To break the habit, you will need to hurt both emotionally and physically while you are learning the new tool of sobriety. How long? Everyone is different. Some adjust fairly quickly while others seem to have a more difficult time with it. One of the major factors will be the length of time you spent drinking or using drugs. This is why you need a support group and meaningful relationships.

Steve's Story

Steve's girlfriend, Jean, a fictitious name, was what is considered to be a "maintenance drinker." What this means is that she would drink an average of two beers an hour all day long from the moment she would get up in the morning until she would go to sleep (pass out) at night. She would maintain her blood alcohol level at a steady rate. If her Blood/Alcohol Content would get low, she would experience withdrawals in the form of sweats and nausea. Jean was truly addicted to beer.

Her relationship with her boyfriend, Steve, had lasted 3 years until he began to see a need for him to stop drinking and could see what it was doing to Jean and her children. For the first three years, they had consumed alcohol together on a daily basis, both feeling sorry for themselves and for the injustices that life seemed to have bestowed upon them. The only thing they really had in common was their reliance on alcohol and sex, another form of escape and feelings of pleasure that they would confuse for happiness. Consequently, their sexual activity was just as abundant as their drinking.

Jean's boyfriend began to see his own use of alcohol as the cause of his current unhappiness. He had once been in a position where everything he did was successful. Now, he was seeing everything he did to either fail or never materialize. Looking back on his past accomplishments, he asked himself, 'what am I doing differently today that I wasn't doing back then?' The answer became clear. He was not drinking a fifth of Scotch every day as he had been the last several years. It was then that he had his first revelation about his own alcohol use.

Meanwhile, Jean began to sense that she was losing Steve. She began to notice a difference in his attitude about drinking and he began to start talking and thinking like someone who didn't drink all the time as she did. She knew very well how people behaved who didn't drink or abuse alcohol. To her, non-drinkers or non-abusers were not to be trusted because they would eventually begin to get on her case about her own drinking. She began to compensate for his lack of drinking and change of thinking by increasing her sexual activities with him . . . thinking that would help to keep him in her world. Their sexual episodes were phenomenal to say the least.

As time passed, Steve saw that he needed to quit drinking and get his life back in order. He was sick and tired of being tired and sick from all of the drinking. He decided to quit his consumption of alcohol. The effect this had on Jean was for her to withdraw from Steve. He was now becoming a threat to her alcohol use merely by his decision to quit. She began to feel guilty about her drinking . . . not that she hadn't before. But now, because Steve was no longer drinking, his non-use made her use more evident in her eyes. Steve didn't have to talk to Jean about her drinking, and he didn't. But the more he continued to not drink, the more she saw her own use as problematic and didn't want to have to face it.

Alcoholics and addicts are like that. They don't want to see or hear anything about their use of drugs or alcohol from anyone, including them. They already know they have a problem but they don't want to have to admit it. When anyone talks to them about it, they are showing them real world images of themselves which are in direct opposition of their Quality World images of themselves. They become defensive and see and hear everything that is said about their use as being criticized, blamed, complained about, nagging them, punishing them, threatening them, and in some cases, being bribed if they would stop.

Did this make Jean stop drinking? On the contrary she began drinking more. She even began hiding her drinking from Steve to make him think that she was either not drinking or cutting down. But Steve was not that gullible to not see her motives and ploys. The more Steve continued to not drink, the healthier he began to get. He started setting goals, making plans, and getting his life in order. Was he a cured alcoholic? Not by a long shot. He was only a dry drunk.

Steve continued to think like an alcoholic in some areas of his life i.e. he believed that if he quit drinking, Jean would see the need to stop drinking as well. WRONG. He believed that their fantastic sexual experiences would be enough to convince Jean to stop drinking for fear that she would lose, "The best" she had ever known. WRONG.

Soon, Steve found himself on the brink of upward mobility. He knew that he could no longer be associated with Jean and her drinking while associating with those he needed in order to further advance his business life and personal life. As politely and as cautiously as he could, he informed Jean that he was moving on into a world where their past use of alcohol together would not be seen as favorable and that it would hold him back. He also explained that if they were to continue in their relationship, that he could not be accepted in business circles when he had a girlfriend who was drinking all day and night long. "What you do," he said, "is your choice. I'll not tell you to stop drinking. If you do, it will be because you wanted to and not because I wanted you to." (This is NOT Choice Theory. Steve was trying to get Jean to change by disguising the seven deadly habits of criticizing, threatening, and bribing all in very subtle ways). All he succeeded in doing was to say things that Jean perceived him as saying to her, "you're a drunk and if you don't stop, I'm moving on." All of her shame and guilt began to show up.

Again, Steve did not understand the power of addiction. He was certain that she would stop drinking because she loved him and wanted him in her life. When it comes to an addiction, the addiction will win most of the time.

People can get very creative when they don't get their needs met . . .especially their addictive needs. Jean always had a heavy supply of beer in her garage. Instead of keeping six or more of them in the refrigerator at a time, when Steve quit drinking, she began to keep only one beer in the refrigerator. Her intention was to fool Steve into thinking that she was no longer drinking and that if he could do it, so could she. He was supposed to notice that every time he would open the refrigerator, he would see a can of beer sitting where it had been for days on end. But Steve was not mentally retarded and he was a lot sharper now that he was no longer drinking. It became apparent that Jean would drink the one beer behind Steve's back and then quickly replace it with another one from the garage.

Jean found a non-alcoholic brand of beer that closely resembled the markings on the can of beer that she preferred. She would openly drink the non-alcoholic beer, putting it in Steve's sight during the day. Then at night, she would drink her regular alcoholic brand but keep her hand wrapped around it so he could not notice that it was the beer with alcohol . . . or so she thought. Steve had no trouble noticing what she was drinking and when she was drinking it. Do normal drinkers resort to such behaviors?

When Jean found those creative ways not to be effective, she began going out alone to drink instead of drinking at home. She found someone else at one of the bars with whom she didn't feel guilty about drinking when she was around him. She broke off her relationship with Steve. Her new partner may not have been as good a sexual partner but he was good enough and she could continue to drink without feeling bad or guilty about it.

Steve began drinking again to deal with his loss, but not for very long. Old habits are hard to break. He quickly concluded that what he was doing by drinking was ridiculous and that he needed to get his life back on track. He did. He went on to become successful in a new business venture and Jean continued to drink. He decided not to look back and to this day, does not know if she is still alive or dead because of her alcohol use. He stopped associating with all of the friends they shared in common. He began to associate with those who were successful. He began to observe the way non alcoholics thought and behaved. Steve improved his life by getting off of alcohol, changing his friends, going to A.A., and started his own business which has become the most successful thing he has accomplished in his life to date. He now has over 18 years of sobriety and reports that it seems like only yesterday that he was caught up in the grip of addiction that ultimately brought him to his knees. He reports the greatest "High" he has ever encountered is the high he gets by being sober and happy each and every day. So there IS success after addiction. And there IS failure in addiction. While it seems like only yesterday that he got sober, he reports that he has no idea of what went on in his life the 8 years he had been drinking. "It's like I went to a party and didn't wake up for 8 years."

Steve would not have made his choices to improve his life had he not evaluated what he wanted in life. He then compared the real world of what he had to his quality world of what he wanted. He had to admit his drinking was a problem and keeping him from his happiness and success. He had tried several times in the past to cut down or even stop on his own but would fail after only two weeks of trying. Nothing he was doing to get his life back was working so he realized that he had to find some new ways that would be more effective.

By giving up on his drinking, he reports he was able to save money to help buy things he needed to improve his life, not cover it up with alcohol. He reports that being sober allowed him to see things so much more clearly that he could see the things he needed to do to become successful. He noticed all of his past friends were miserable and not successful in their relationships or careers, and that they would always get together to commiserate or boast about their upcoming successes that never seemed to materialize. In less than two years, Steve, who had no credit rating, no credit cards, no money to speak of, a beat up 12 year old Cadillac, clothes he had been wearing for years, and no friends, finally had turned it all around and went back to school, changed careers, got reliable transportation, bought new clothes, got credit cards and made sure they were paid each month, made new friends, and . . . bought a brand new home. He stated, "There was no way I could have seen a need to even do those things, much less get them, while I was drinking. It wasn't until I saw a need to quit and realized that it was the alcohol in my life and no satisfying relationships that was causing all of my unhappiness did things start to change in my life. . . and they're STILL changing."

"We were all $25.00 Millionaires," Steve would say. "We would all gather around our favorite bar with our Cadillacs, Jaguars, Mercedes, and Porsches parked outside; wearing our expensive suits, talking about how our next sale or deal would bring us millions of dollars, buying one another drinks all night long, when in actuality we had holes in our socks and underwear. We were in hock up to our eyeballs with mortgages, car payments, and credit card debt and lucky if we had $25.00 to our name. Alcohol kept us in a world of fantasy and not a world of reality.

As a follow up to this story, Steve relates the time he decided to go back to his old watering hole after a year of avoiding it, to see how the old gang was doing . . . if anything had changed in their lives. He reports that when he walked into the bar, the same old faces were gathered at the same old place at the end of the bar. "When they saw me, someone yelled, 'Hey, there's Steve! Get over here you old sonofabitch. Where you been keepin' yourself?'

Steve told them that he had gone back to school and had started his own business. Steve was particularly interested in how negative the old gang was in their thoughts when he was asked, "Are you going for your Master's degree?"

"I just might," said Steve.

"Hell, you'll be 50 years old when you get your Master's degree."

Steve said, "I'm going to be 50 whether I get my Master's degree or not. What does my age have to do with it?"

Then the group offered to buy Steve a drink. When the bartender arrived, Steve ordered a cup of coffee. One of the group members who was willing to pay for Steve's drink said, "Fuck you, man! I'm not paying for a cup of coffee. Order a goddamn drink!" Steve looked at the group of people he had not seen for the last year and suddenly saw a group of pathetic, unhappy people who were not his friends at all. They were willing to pay $4.50 for a cocktail for him but not .50 cents for a cup of coffee.

Steve could now see that these were not his friends. They were only people who enjoyed his company as long as he drank alcohol with them. If he didn't drink with them, they didn't see him as much of a friend. Steve stated, "I turned around and walked out the door and never went back."

Who are the people in your life whom you have lost due to your drinking or drug use? Now ask yourself, who are the **important** people in your life that you lost and would like to have back in your life? Write their names on a piece of paper.

Now put them in order of importance to you. How many of them are not deceased and still available to rekindle the friendship if you knew how to do it? By that, I don't mean that you want to remarry your ex-wife when she's already married to someone else.

Is it necessary to rekindle old relationships? Not necessarily. If they are important people to you then I would say yes. But if not, why not start over with a whole new group of people. I recommend you associate with people who are happy and as successful as you would like to be. You will acquire a lot of wisdom and guidance from alcoholics and addicts who have several years of recovery and have become successful. I also highly recommend that you associate with people who have NEVER abused or have been addicted to drugs or alcohol. You will find a lot of healthier attitudes, ways to cope, and ways to perceive things with "Normies" as well as with recovering people.

If you don't have anyone to put on your list, then you are better off than you thought you were. ANYONE you meet from today forward has potential for being a non-obligatory friend.

Call someone up from the past that you haven't talked to in a long time. Call them during normal hours and not at 3:30 AM as you would have done when you were drunk. Just make sure it isn't someone who has taken the same road you did with drugs or alcohol. This is not as uncommon as one might think. I recall phoning an old friend who used to scold me terribly for smoking cigarettes. Once in awhile I would kid him by offering him a cigarette knowing he would get upset if I did. He used to grab my pack of cigarettes, twist them in a knot and throw them in the trash.

While I was going through my own recovery, I decided to give him a call in the hope of rekindling an old friendship. We made small talk, briefly brought each other up to date on our past separate lives, and then made arrangements to meet for dinner. He originally wanted to meet at a bar but I told him that I was in the process of giving up alcohol and didn't want to go to anyplace that might be slippery territory for me. He understood.

We had a great time over dinner and afterward, while walking to our cars, he reached in his shirt pocket and pulled out a joint and offered it to me. I couldn't believe my eyes. Here was a guy who would throw away a brand new pack of cigarettes if I ever offered him one and now he was smoking pot. Once again, we parted company and we never got back together. I later found out that he had contracted lung cancer.

What can you do for the sake of the relationship that you want to improve? If you are like most alcoholics/addicts, you have a history of past drug or alcohol use that has driven the important people in your life from you. Not only are you the bad guy here, but they, too, played a role that seriously harmed the relationship by imposing all of the seven deadly habits of external control on you. You have both been using external control on each other and the result is where you both are today in your relationships with one another.

You see them as someone who doesn't respect you and you would be right. Who wants to respect someone who has done all of the things you did when using or drinking? They see you as someone who doesn't respect them and you see them as someone who doesn't respect you. So you're both guilty of the harmed relationship. However, it's not your place to remind them of their part in it. It's only important for you to see YOUR part in the harmed relationship. Learn the habit of NOT doing any of the seven deadly habits ever again with anyone in your life, be they family, spouse, coworker, teacher, or a mere acquaintance.

You may have told them that you are working on quitting your alcohol or drug use but no matter how often you tell them, they aren't going to believe you. You can also apologize for all of the things that you recognize that you did to harm the relationship but you also need to know that they don't have to accept your apology. You, on the other hand, need to apologize whether they accept your apology or not. This is a part of ridding yourself of your shame and guilt.

If others don't accept your apology, you have only the choice to move on with your own life because you are the only one whom you can control. If they are unwilling, that is their choice. Wish them well and move on. You did what you had to do for yourself. A word to the wise about apologizing to people that you may have harmed in the past. Be selective about whom you choose to do this with. Be savvy enough to realize that you should not apologize to someone for something that you did that might cause them to choose to react in a manner that would not be good for your or their physical wellbeing. For example: Don't apologize to an ex-friend for sleeping with his wife when he didn't know about it in the first place. You can imagine what could happen next. Make amends only with the important people in your life.

God and Higher Power

Religion is not a topic that I do in my usual group therapy sessions because of the variety of clients that I have. Some are agnostic and some are atheistic, but the majorities have some modicum of a religious belief system. So to avoid any controversy as well as shutting down the minds of non-believers, I simply do not go there in group.

But here, I can do what I've always wanted to do: Include God in my book of Choice Theory and Addiction. Choice Theory is not a religious tenet or a religion itself. Choice Theory, however, does fit in with and is compatible with many other concepts. If you are one of those individuals who have no religious beliefs, you may, if you so choose, skip this chapter. Or, you may read it and find something in this section that could really assist you in your quest for achieving sobriety or getting clean and sober. You have everything to gain and nothing to lose by staying with this chapter.

The primary basis of utilizing Choice Theory to overcome your addiction is in the creation of meaningful relationships. It is extremely important that you have at least one, preferably more, non-obligatory relationship in your life right now. One of the best forms that I know of to reestablish a non-obligatory relationship is a relationship with God. Even normal non-drinking/drugging people who have trouble creating relationships with others have found happiness and success in life through their relationship with God.

If you have a background in any faith and have lost it over the years, for whatever reason, revert back to your younger days in your earlier beliefs about God. Bill W., the creator of A.A., liked God. He just didn't like the people who dished it out in the form of ministers, priests, or other forms of clergy. It became an important part of his 12-step program which he would refer to God as your Higher Power, or to God "as YOU know Him."

Studies have been conducted over the years that always seem to come to the same conclusion: The happiest people are those who possess a strong belief and faith in God. It doesn't have to be a Christian God either. It can be whatever religious belief you subscribe to. For those of you who have fallen away from your faith, more than likely, you did so for any number of reasons. Perhaps you merely stopped practicing your faith and decided it was not a part of your life that you needed. Or, you got fed up with those who you perceive were hypocrites or who you felt were forcing religion on you, or criticized you and labeled you as a sinner, preaching fire and brimstone, etc. Your own use of drugs or alcohol may be why you dropped away, feeling hypocritical yourself.

I used to say, religion is for people who are afraid of going to hell. Spirituality is for people who have been there. One without the other, religion and spirituality, is weak and one needs the support of the other. The problem I see with those who have fallen away after they once believed is that they just didn't know how to use it. They had a tendency to revert to their religion only during times when unhappy things were happening in their lives and gave it no thought during the happier times. Then they would say, "Where was God when I needed Him?"

In order for your faith to work effectively, you must include God all of the time in your life. Begin the day with God. Take a break during the day with God. And end the day with God. I have had people say to me, "Prove to me God exists." And I would say, 'Prove to me that He doesn't?' Faith is just that . . . faith. We don't call our religion Fact. Faith is the belief in something that has no definite proof of existence or in the outcome.

Am I a religious fanatic --one who professes my faith openly all the time to others? Not at all. I'll be more than happy to discuss it with anyone should they wish to discuss it but I don't go around preaching my faith. This book chapter is the closest I've ever come to doing that. The actual stories of others who have connected or reconnected with their belief in God to help them overcome their addictions can be found in most every A.A. publication you can find. There are also those who testify to their success in overcoming their obstacles in Churches and the Salvation Army.

So here's my story and how I applied it to my benefit:

I was raised Catholic. I had even entertained the thought of becoming a priest when I was younger. I went to parochial school and to Mass six days a week for eight years. I was an altar boy for 4 years. I grew up in the Catholic faith when Mass was still conducted in Latin. I changed my mind on the priest thing when I discovered girls. It wasn't until I was 24 years old, stuck in an Army barracks in a blizzard in Fairbanks, Alaska on a Sunday morning that I missed going to Sunday Mass for the first time in my life. I was actually shocked to discover that a lightening bolt did not come down from the heavens and strike me dead, as I was practically led to believe would happen when younger. After that experience, as well as having a few experiences that didn't work out whenever I called upon God for His help, I decided that I didn't really need God or religion in my life anymore. I still believed in God, I just didn't go to church or pray anymore. I still held onto my basic belief system that a God did truly have to exist based upon the incredible order of the universe and all forms of life and our ecosystem on our planet. And there were times when I would even doubt His existence when I didn't get what I wanted in life.

What I didn't realize until later is that God does, indeed, hear all of our prayers and sometimes, His answer is, "No." After several years of giving God little to no attention in my life, I had begun to amass, as all of us do, several of life's unhappy experiences. Some people blame God for them. My ego was never that large to think that God had nothing better to do than to make Mike Rice's life miserable. But over the years of failed relationships and a failed marriage, I eventually ended up in a bottle to deal with all of my unhappiness. It was the only tool that I had at the time to deal with it. And since I would always feel miserable after I quit drinking, I found that all I had to do was keep drinking to avoid feeling miserable.

After five years of drinking daily and nightly, not only did my relationships not get any better, they got worse. I found myself drawn to others in my life that had the same tools I had to deal with unhappiness . . . alcohol. Their lives were not any better than mine and we would find ourselves drawing one another down in the muck and mire of misery and further unhappiness. Other areas of my life were suffering as much as my relationships were. Steady employment didn't exist. I would keep changing careers, looking for something that might have a big payoff. Alcoholics are grandiose thinkers. We think big but have short pockets and little knowledge to tackle large projects.

One Saturday night, after having basically passed out on my bed, still dressed and leaving the TV in my bedroom on all night; I began hearing voices. I could tell they weren't voices of a hallucinogenic type. I was not asleep nor was I awake. I was in that area of consciousness that I refer to as the nether zone . . . halfway between awake and asleep.

I listened to the voice. It was a man's voice and whatever he was saying had grabbed me in the nether zone. To this day, I couldn't tell you what it is that he said but whatever it was, it was something that I needed to hear at that particular time in my life. I had left the TV on all night and the voice was coming from the TV. I didn't want to fully wake up and see who it was. I just wanted to listen. And as I listened, his words were hitting home and moving me spiritually and motivating me to do something with my life.

To add even more drama to the story, my bedroom had a cathedral ceiling and the window on my East wall was an arched window one might see in a church but without any stained glass. The speaker then said something that told me that I had to do something about my life and do it now or I was in for more unhappiness and sorrow than I would ever know. He brought me to, and showed me, my "bottom." I sat up to see who it was who had stirred me enough to start taking back control of my life and saw that it was Dr. Robert H. Schuller from the Hour of Power television ministry. Just as I sat up, the sun moved across my window and a ray of sunlight from the church-like window moved across my body as I lay in bed. A sense of peace and calmness came over me like I had never felt before. It was my time to exhale and feel the weight of all of my problems melt away by seeing the need to stop doing what I subconsciously knew was one of my problems (my drinking) and to take back control of my life instead of feeling sorry for myself and blaming others for my bad luck.

Later, I discovered a video of "My Name Is Bill W." (A film about how A.A. got started), with actors James Woods and James Garner. In the video, a scene very much like the experience I had with the sunlight across my bed and the feeling of peace and serenity came to Bill Wilson. I show this video often to my groups and each time the scene comes up where Bill is in his hospital bed and the sunlight shines on him bringing him calmness and peace, the hair on the back of my neck stands up and I get an instant flashback to my own similar experience.

That story I just related to you happened 18 years ago and to this day, I have only missed the Hour of Power program on Sunday mornings perhaps 7 or 8 times only because I was out of town and it wasn't showing on the local stations where I was. Even with my new awareness of what I had to do to begin to pull myself up, it wasn't until several years later that I came to realize how to use God in my life to make it all come together. This was due to my own slow realization and not due to a natural course of events. So now I am able to pass it along to you, for those of you who can use it, to get your life where it should be and you won't have to wait a long time before it happens. Here's how it works:

Whether or not you realize it, your higher power, or God, or Allah, or Yahweh, or Buddha is always with you. The key to working with God is to be thankful for all of the blessings and grace that has been bestowed to you. And if you have a hard time listing these blessings, then you need to start looking at yourself and your life differently than you have. It is near impossible to see the grace of God if you are the possessor of anger towards others or if you place yourself in the role of a victim.

You're alive. You have talents - whether or not you are using them, that's another story. You have people in your life that care about you. Hopefully, you have a bed, a place to stay, a job, clothes, a home, furniture, any material belongings, etc. If you don't have many of these things, just think about how excited you're going to be as your Higher Power begins to bless you with them.

Be thankful even for the bad things that have happened to you in your life. Sound crazy? It is. But for every adversity you have in life, something equally as good or better will come from it if you look for the positive side instead of the negative side. I never would have become a therapist if I hadn't become a drunk first.

God has plans for you. He always has. You just haven't been in touch with Him to learn what it is. As long as you drink or use drugs, all of the directions you will receive from your Higher Power will not be recognized or heard.

Pray! Pray out of gratitude for all that you have and for all that you are going to have. Start your day with prayer . . . for God to send the person that He wants you to see and talk to today. There may be someone who needs your help or someone who will help you. Pray for God to show you the direction He wants you to go in your life. Look at the things you are good at doing and the things that you like to do. Somewhere, somehow, there are people making money doing those things. How can you use them to earn a living? What do you have to do in order to make it happen? What's stopping you from doing them? Every obstacle we experience in life is meant to teach us something. Many people stop or give up with any obstacles instead of looking at what it is that they have to learn from the situation.

God knows what your needs are. You don't have to pray for them. Instead, pray for what you can do today or tomorrow to make someone else's life better. In A.A., we have a saying. (We have lots of sayings in A.A.) If you want to keep it (your sobriety and happiness), you have to give it away. Help others the way you found help. Bill W. found his sobriety by helping others to stay sober.

I'm reminded of the story of the man who was caught up in a flood. The fire department came by in a fire truck before the water reached his home and offered to take him to safety. He replied, "No thanks. I'll put my trust in the Lord to take care of me." The flood waters rose and the man had to move to the second story of his home. Some people came by in a boat and offered to take him to safety. He said, "No thanks. I'm putting my faith in the Lord to save me." The waters rose even higher and he had to climb to the roof of his home. A helicopter flew overhead and offered to take him to safety. He replied, "Thanks, but I'll rely on the Lord to save me." The water rose higher and the man was swept off of his roof and he drowned. He found himself in heaven and when he saw God, he said, "I put all of my faith in you to save me and you let me down." God said, "Let you down? I sent you a fire truck, a boat, and a helicopter and you turned them all away."

God feeds all of the birds in the world but He doesn't throw their food in their nest. You must start taking responsibility for your own behavior and for your own future. No one is going to do it for you. And while we're at it, you can not do it alone. I have read the biographies of many people over the years and one thing that I have found out about them is that none of them became successful without the help of others. Asking for help is not a sign of weakness. It's a sign of intelligence. If you don't know how to do something that you need to know, ASK someone. If you need help getting something done, ASK someone to help you. If your attitude is one of "If you want something done right, you gottta do it yourself," you need an attitude check.

Not only is doing everything yourself a bad idea, you won't have time to do the other things that need to be done.

For the Christians out there: Were you not taught that Christ died on the cross so that your sins will be forgiven? If you are a Christian and you don't believe that, then that would be a slap in the face of the person who was tormented, scourged, ridiculed, and crucified and all for nothing. The next time you start to feel sorry for yourself, look what Christ had to go through. All of the people who praised Him when He entered Jerusalem were the same people who yelled out to have Him crucified. He was abandoned by his disciples and even Peter denied knowing Him. He was accused of being a blasphemer, a charlatan, and an evil person when all He did was teach people how to love one another. He was wrongly accused of all of his crimes and beaten with whips that tore His flesh. He was crowned in mockery with a crown of thorns. He was marched through the streets in public humiliation and nailed to a cross to die a slow and painful death. And what was His crime? How to love God and one another. And you think life or someone else has handed YOU a raw deal?

For all of you martyrs out there, we have a saying in recovery: Get down off the cross. There's only room enough for one up there.

Make God, Christ, Allah, Yahweh, or whomever you believe in your best friend. God is always there when you need Him but you have to be in tune with God to be aware of His presence. God loves you and forgives you regardless of any or all of your indiscretions. If God can forgive you, why can't you forgive yourself? Are you more powerful than God?

God knows what you need. You don't have to pray to Him for it. You only need to praise and thank Him for what you have and for direction for the plans He has for you each day. Prayer is a wonderful thing but some people can get totally caught up in it with expectations for their results. Then when they don't get what they expected, they get frustrated or even angry. Even God said to Moses, "Moses, stop your praying and get your people moving." (Exodus 14:15) In other words, take action. Do something besides pray.

Personally, I can't think of anyone else whom I would want as my best friend than Christ. After that, I would want my wife on the list. After that, I would want my friends that I work with and others outside of my personal life on the list. And if I didn't have anyone on my list at all, except for Christ, I'd still be in great shape. The more meaningful relationships you have, the happier you will be. The more meaningful relationships you have the better your odds for kicking your habits.

Perhaps the greatest advantage of having God, as you know Him, in your life is to deal with your shame and guilt. The two most important elements of acquiring and maintaining sobriety and being clean from drugs are to 1.) Rid yourself of shame and guilt and 2.) Acquire meaningful relationships.

God can and will forgive us our sins, no matter how horrific they may be. And if you have a hard time striking up new and healthy relationships, start out with God.

What If I Don't Believe in God?

If this is your belief then you have three choices: Find ways to start believing, recognize some form of higher power that is more powerful than you are, or keep on denying that God exists. But if you find your life is not where you would like it to be, how has not believing in God helped your life improve? Has not believing in God helped you in your relationships with others? What have you got to lose by making an attempt at believing? If you're like many addicts/alcoholics, God is the only person willing to come into your life right about now. Who else do you have?

Yes, you can get clean and sober without God in your life. Anything is possible. But how happy will you be? Why limit your support system to mere mortals, if that? You can choose how you will react and live life each and every day.

I have often heard in A.A. and other circles that you can make anything your higher power i.e. a doorknob or a coffee cup. I'm sorry, but I can't make that one work for me. I have had a whole bunch of coffee cups and doorknobs in my home when I was drinking and yet my life and marriage and career still went down the drain.

I have heard some people say, "I can't believe anything that I can't see" or "there is no proof that God exists." I can't see the electricity in the wires in my home but I have faith it is there and the proof is when I use any electric appliance. Belief in God is called "Faith." It isn't called "Fact." Faith means there is no proof other than your personal belief.

Do you believe in evil? If so, then you must believe in good. To have evil without good would not make evil, evil or good, good. You can't have light without dark. Do you believe in negative energy? If so, then you would have to believe in positive energy. For whatever power you can think of there must be a higher power if there is a lower power. If you can claim this concept then you can believe in your form of higher power . . . a power greater than yourself that has the ability to make positive things happen as well as a negative power that makes negative things happen. Which power would you want to adhere to in your life, your higher power or lower power? Which power do you think would bring you more happiness in your life?

Forgiving Yourself

Assignment Three

This topic coincides with all of my past references to Shame and Guilt. I can not think of anyone, other than God, who has not done some things in their life that they were sorry for later. Everyone has something from their past that they would just as soon not have anyone else know. In fact, hiding your past from others takes a lot of energy and effort to not be discovered. Another saying we have in recovery, (we have tons of sayings) is: We're as sick as our secrets.

None of us is perfect. We are mortal human beings. Making mistakes is major part of our being. It is also one of the ways we learn not to make them by doing them over and over. Some people are slow learners.

Regardless of your addictions, one will not possess or experience happiness or sobriety for very long as long as they possess shame and guilt in their life.

The first person you must want to change is the only person in your life whom you can control who can change: YOU! If you don't like you, how can you expect anyone else to like you? If you don't like you, why should you even bother to change? (That's what you've been thinking all along). You desperately want others to like you but you don't like yourself. So you go through life drinking or drugging so you can "be somebody." In other words, you can laugh, joke around, project yourself as happy and even successful while putting on airs all along. . . Faking it -- trying to be something that you aren't.

A truly genuine person is someone who accepts who and what s/he is. They are human beings, not human doings. How has your opinion of yourself helped you in acquiring meaningful relationships? How has seeing yourself as a seriously flawed individual helped you in getting clean and sober? Do the successful and happy people that you see in life use drugs and alcohol to get successful? How do you see yourself? Can you see yourself as a truly successful and happy person who is drunk or stoned most of the day? Does that image take you to the degree of happiness and success in life that you would like to possess? How far up from "miserable" would you like to be?

You may accept the fact that you are an addict or alcoholic, or someone who is addicted to an addict or alcoholic but I'm sure you don't see yourself as happy in any of those images.

Assignment Four

Let's take a look at your quality values in your quality world. What is important to you? Take a moment and make a list of all of the things you can think of that make up your values. This exercise is not as difficult as you may think. I'll help you get started. They are usually found in the areas of things that you want to have in yourself as well as others. They don't have to be in any special order.

- Fairness
- Honesty
- Love
- Peace of mind
- Health
- Gratitude
- Acceptance and respect from others

If you were to come across someone who was down and out and in need of any of these values (my list or yours, either one), what would you say to them in order that they might acquire the ability to be fair, honest, loving, to others? What would they need to do to find love in their life? What would they need to do to acquire peace of mind, health, be grateful, and gain the respect of others?

If they are, indeed, your values, you will know what to tell them. If you can't think of anything to say, then it is doubtful that it is one of your values. So write out, or even say out loud, what you think someone else must do to acquire any one of these values. Then take a look at yourself. How many of the things that you say one must do to have and maintain this value are you doing? They were once your values so they meant something to you. You can reacquire them by making them your values once again. Just do what you would tell someone else to do to possess them.

Here is usually where I hear someone say, "But you don't know what I've done in my life. I've really done some horrible things. I can't possibly forgive myself for that. I don't want to be a hypocrite." You'll only be a hypocrite if you believe one thing and do another. So get back to your beliefs and values and make a sincere effort to stop doing the things that would make you a hypocrite.

FORGIVE YOURSELF! You're human. Humans make mistakes. There isn't a human on the face of the earth who hasn't. Whatever you have done in the past is done . . . over. You can't go back and change any part of it. But one thing you can do is forgive yourself and never do it again. The only thing you could do that would be unforgiving would be if you continue to do the things that make you feel badly about yourself. . . things that not only harm others, but yourself as well.

Do you deserve to be happy? There are many people in life in their addictions who would say "no" to that question. This would be an indicator of just how deep they are in their addiction. But even those who would say no are also those who would like to say "yes." Happiness, my friends, is an inside job. We don't get it from others. It's a choice. Others may help us in certain quests for pleasure but they will not provide us with happiness unless we see them favorably and they give meaning to our own life. And that emotion comes from within us, not from others. And so it goes, if you can't forgive yourself, why should anyone else? They won't until you do.

Relationships

Creating new or reconnecting with past relations is an integral part of sobriety and happiness. The first person you need to reconnect with is you. Earlier, you may recall that I spoke about the dangers of getting involved in relationships with others whom you may meet in A.A. and thirteen steppin.' The relationships I want to speak about now are those where there are no romantic or sexual aspects to the relationship. To have any type of successful relationship, whether it is romantic or platonic, you need to have a good relationship with yourself. If you don't like yourself, why should anyone else?

For the last several months or years, you have been beating yourself up for all of your past and current screw-ups. But even more than what you have been doing to yourself, others have done even more. Just look at all of the important people in your life that you had or who are about to take you out of their quality world.

They have applied ample amounts of the seven deadly habits of external control on a regular basis for so long that you are starting to echo their sentiments about yourself. Not only do you feel as if everyone is against you, but you are against yourself as well.

If you have stopped ingesting alcohol or your drug of choice, this is the chapter that will assist you in keeping off of the drug, maintain your sobriety, and finding the happiness you have been longing to have for much of your life.

You have read it before throughout this book but it bears repeating over and over again. You can only find happiness through meaningful relationships with the important people in your life and that can only be achieved by learning new ways in dealing with yourself and others. The relationships you need in recovery are the repaired relationships with the important people in your life and preferably, not past sexual relationships (unless it is your current spouse); your sponsor; someone who is happy and successful and has never had an addiction problem; your friends that you meet at A.A. If you are single, don't go looking for new love interests just yet. You have a lot of recovery to do before you can effectively begin a healthy love relationship.

There are specific policies you will need to adhere to in dealing with yourself and others:

1. The only person you can control is yourself.

2. The only person other people can control is themselves, even though they will try to control you and others.

3. Since you can not control others, let others do what they do and don't you get caught up in what they are doing. Don't make their "stuff" your "stuff."

4. You will need to start with yourself before you can maintain healthy relationships with others.

Creating long lasting relationships will be the result of non-obligatory friendships, free from the deadly habits, external control, and beginning use of the healthy habits.

Starting with the first policy: You have been feeling out of control for any number of months or years. The fact is you have more control over yourself than you realize. You have been allowing others to control you by the way you have been reacting to them when they use the deadly habits on you. Eventually, you may have finally detached from them, and perhaps the majority of society, to avoid further unwanted emotions and physical discomfort. Begin learning the power of changing what you want and/or changing how you react when you don't get what you want.

Forgive yourself for any and all past mistakes you have made in your life. More than likely, you have been feeling down on yourself as well as feeling like a victim because of how others have been treating you. If you are a victim, it's because you chose to be a victim. Feeling sorry for yourself is choosing to be a victim. It frees you from having to take responsibility for your own behavior.

I'm not speaking about the person who physically beat you, raped, murdered, or any other horrendous crime that humanity oft performs on others. I'm referring to those whom you feel have abandoned you, criticized you, blamed you, complained about you, punished you, threatened you, nagged you, bribed and rewarded you to get you to do something that you didn't want to do. You have had a choice all of your life on how you could react to these acts against you but you knew no other way than to resort to these behaviors yourself or shrink into submission and allow it to continue to affect you. In other words, you have been giving your power to control yourself away to others to use against you. You have been feeling sorry for yourself with such thoughts as, "Poor me. Poor me. Pour me another drink."

To overcome this part of your self-perception, forgive yourself. Decide right here and now that you are the only one who can control you and that you are going to start to take action by taking responsibility for all that happens to you from this day forward.

Shake the shame and guilt off of yourself. One night, after meeting with my sponsor, he asked me, "Mike, how you would feel if tomorrow morning, you woke up to discover that the headlines on the New York Times stated: MIKE RICE IS AN ALCOHOLIC." I responded, 'I'd be embarrassed to all ends. I'd want to run away and hide so no one could ever find me.' Then he said to me, "who do you know in New York?" 'No one,' I replied. Then he asked, "Who in New York knows you?" I thought for a moment and said, 'there may be someone who now lives in New York who knows me, I don't know.' My sponsor then said, "Most people might pick up the paper, read the headlines and say, 'Who the hell is Mike Rice, and why should I give a shit if he's an alcoholic?'" It was then that I saw that any embarrassment or unwanted emotion that I would experience from the above example would have come strictly from me and not others, and that no one else really cared if I was an alcoholic or not. By choosing those emotions, look what I had been doing to myself. This was an important lesson for me.

How many people do you know who have never made some pretty serious mistakes in their life? Many people go through life as if they have never made any mistakes and are perfect but I'm here to tell you that none of us are perfect and we all have made some grievous errors in our lives.

Now here's the reality of it all: Even those who portray themselves as perfect have done some things in their life that they hope you or anyone else will never discover about them. When your image of yourself in your quality world differs from what it really is in the real world, you will experience frustration and compensate for this unmet need of power and self worth, as well as belonging, by behaving in ways that you have developed over the years to satisfy this need. This is done in any number of ways such as being righteous toward others, arrogant, controlling, defensive, all-knowing, giving the impression that you know what is right for everyone, attention seeking, lying, appearing to be someone or something that you aren't.

Or, you might take the opposite approach such as cowering to others, needing acceptance and shunning all possible abandonment from others by giving in to them for all of their wants and needs instead of your own; fearful of saying "no" to things that you would rather not do because you don't want others to dislike you, acting like Pagliacci and laughing on the outside while crying on the inside.

We're as sick as our secrets. Hiding all of our past errors and negative perceptions of ourselves from others is a full-time job. It takes a lot of energy to be constantly on guard to protect our secrets. So how does one overcome all of this? Simply by not having anymore secrets. Admit to yourself and another person whom you trust, a non-obligatory person, those things you have done that you may be ashamed of. This is the 5th Step in A.A. The other person's role is not to judge you but to allow you to vent and admit that you're not a perfect person and have made some mistakes that you don't intend to ever do again. See the important of having meaningful relationships? And this is only just a start. If you have a strong connection with your religious faith, admit your errors to God or another higher power.

Most religions have a forgiving God rather than an opposing, damning God. If God can give His Son up to be crucified so that your sins may be forgiven, then the least

174

you can do is to be able to forgive yourself as well. Since God has forgiven you and you find it difficult to forgive yourself, then who is it that made you more powerful than God?

There is nothing that you have done that you can not be forgiven by others, yourself, or by God. And it only takes two of the three to be successful. If others fail or refuse to forgive you, then move on with your life.

Before I had gone back to school to become a therapist, I had come up with the concept that I felt only God had presented to me to use that would change me and the world. It was a concept that I just sort of got from the Universe. No one told it to me. I didn't read it anywhere. It was mine and only mine. I felt so strongly positive about it that I was going to share it with the world and I just knew in my heart of hearts that it would revolutionize the world. Here is the concept that I came up with:

We are actually three people in one;

1. How we see ourselves
2. How we want others to see us
3. How we really are

I would write each of these personalities inside an individual circle, side by side. And then I would profoundly claim: "To be a truly genuine and authentic person, all three of these circles need to be inside one complete circle, where all three are one and the same.

I hadn't been is school for very long when one of my classes that was teaching all of the different modalities of therapy showed me that none of my concepts were an original idea. Some of this stuff had been around since before the days of Christ. Even Freud (Geiwitz 1976) had the Id, the Ego, and Super Ego. Burns (1967) had the Parent, The Adult, and The Child. Even Luft and Ingham (1955) had their famous Johari window concept long before I had my perception of three people in one. Was I disappointed? A little. But I decided that I came up with my concept on my own so I must be on the right track in some areas of human behavior.

Forgive yourself! Release all of your secrets and feel the weight of the world lift from your shoulders. Be able to breathe again and live life without having to look over your shoulder all the time to protect your secrets. I can tell you that since having done this myself, I feel like my life is an open book. I'm not proud of many things that I have done in my lifetime. But if you ask me about something specific from my past, I will probably tell you. That does not mean that I willingly go around disclosing any or all of my indiscretions. It just means I am willing to tell you the truth and not hide things anymore. Refer to steps 5, 6, & 7 for those of you who are working the 12 steps of A.A.

Trust others. This is a difficult thing for some people to do. I'll make it short and sweet: Trust anyone and everyone unless they give you reason not to. Yes, there are those whom you have never personally met but you may have a gut feeling that they are not to be trusted because of their behavior and expressions. To this I say, go with your gut feelings. You have them for a reason and most of the time, they are right.

The second part of creating and maintaining meaningful relationships has to do with not ever doing anything to try to control another person even though they may do otherwise to you. When others choose to put external control into play and use the seven deadly habits, you can choose to perceive their behavior as nothing more than "Noise." And like noise, you can choose to react to it negatively or indifferently. If you react negatively, would you feel happier or would it make you feel badly? If you react to the external control of others, would that help you get closer in your relationship with others or drive you further apart?

Mike came to me to deal with anger issues that stemmed from his divorce from his ex-wife and the children they had. After what he described as a nasty divorce, he realized that he had these children in his life and that he needed to maintain his relationship with them.

"I would call in an effort to speak to my kids after the divorce and when my ex wife heard my voice, she would immediately go into her attack mode and call me names and blame me for the marriage ending when it was she who had the affair and filed for divorce."

"All she had to do was call me a name and I would do a knee-jerk reaction and I would yell back, "F*** YOU!" Then he would slam the phone down on the cradle. This behavior would occur at least twice a month when Mike would try to connect with his children. Then it came to Mike that both his and his ex-wife's behavior was not anything that he wanted his children to be witnessing. So Mike reached into his tool kit to solve the problem. Mike admitted that he didn't have too many effective tools at that time in his life. The only tool he found that was effective for ending the unwanted behavior was to simply "Not call anymore." And it worked. His children no longer witnessed their parents acting like they were out of control.

Several months passed and it occurred to Mike that while there was no more name calling, blaming, criticizing, etc., his children were growing up and he was not around to see it or be a part of it. He decided to call his wife in an attempt to speak with his kids and didn't care what she would say or do for him to get to do this. He reports the conversation sent like this:

Mike: "Hello, Sally?"

Sally: "You sonofabitch.!

Mike: "I've been called that before."

Sally: "You just f***ed everything up."

Mike: "I have a habit of doing that it would appear."

Sally: "Everything you touch turns to shit!"

Mike: (He wanted to say, 'I know. I touched you and look what happened.' But he didn't"). He said, "Yeah, it seems like that's the way my life has been going lately."

No matter what Sally said to Mike, he didn't react as he had in the past. Sally quickly found herself playing a one-sided game . . .a game that takes two people to play. And since she was the only one playing, it wasn't any fun for her and she quit. Once she quit, Mike asked, "Are the kids there?" Sally said, "yeah, just a minute." And put them on the phone.

Mike had taken advantage of both choices (#1 and #2 as discussed earlier.) He changed what he wanted (to have her stop bitching at him and calling him names) and he changed how he reacted when he didn't get what he wanted from her. The result? What he wanted all along . . . to talk to his children.

You have no right to tell others what they need to do or should be doing unless they ask. And even then, what is right for you may not be right for anyone else. Once we begin thinking and acting like we know what's good for everyone, we start to harm our relationships. Just don't do it. It's that simple. You may know what's right for you and your life but that doesn't mean it is right for others and their life. If you want to distance your relationship with anyone in your life, just start telling them what they need to start doing.

In the course of my travels on airlines, it is not so uncommon that the person sitting next to you on an airline will ask you, "What do you do?" I used to tell them that I am a behavioral therapist, but I no longer do this. Now I tell them that I teach happiness. Before, if I said I was a behavioral therapist, the next response would always seem to come next: "That must be a really hard job because you have to listen to everyone's problems all day." What they don't understand is that, yes, I do listen to their problems but I don't get caught up in their problems. I don't make their problems my problems. This is what many people who are not behavioral therapists do. They try to help by taking on the problems of their friends and family. Then they start telling them what they should or must do based upon what they think they would do if in the same situation. This is a sure-fire way of harming their relationship with that person.

Invariably, after I would explain this to my flying companion, they would bring up the behavior of "a friend" or a family member (meaning themselves) and want free therapy to our final destination.

Following this, the conversation would eventually end up going to the topic of medication and how effective or how ineffective it worked for others that they knew which would have led to explanations that would have taken longer than our flight would take to reach our final destination, including those who would choose to argue points and challenge my approach to behavioral health. Today, I find it much easier to let others believe what they want to believe with no empirical evidence, and I will continue to work and believe what I believe based upon my experience and successes and failures. It is not my job to convince everyone to see their situation in life the same way I see it. If they come to me for help, then I have a right to try to help them by evaluating what they want, what they have been doing, pointing out that what they have been doing may work in some areas but not in others, and helping them to come up with solutions to their problems by trying things that they have not yet tried. If there is a possibility that their medication may be their problem, then we will look at that as well.

This counselor does not believe in brain medications because what we have been calling mental illness has no pathology of any sort and therefore, treating unhappiness with brain meds is no different than drinking alcohol, taking Ecstasy, cocaine, heroin, or any other street drug to deal with their unhappiness. These drugs have no curable properties and may harm the brain permanently rather than provide any cure. But this is another book and a topic that can be further researched by the works of other authors, M.D.s et al in the field of behavioral health that will be listed in the appendix of this book.

I am not so naive to think that every client who comes to me for addiction will be "cured." While I do have a number of clients who have overcome their addictions, I also have clients whose interest was peaked but not enough to effect change. I have also had clients who had definite problems who simply were court-ordered to attend treatment but saw absolutely no need to make any changes in their life. They will become clients again down the road. They weren't ready to hear or do anything that might make their lives better because, in their perceptions, their life was fine and all of their quality world images were being met . . .so far.

In my practice, I rarely tell clients that they can not drink or use drugs. They already know this to be true. The only clients I inform that they can not continue to drink or use are those clients who, if they don't stop, will soon harm themselves or someone else. With the help of self-evaluation, their fantasy of happiness is destroyed and reality sets in.

In all the other alcohol and drug treatment agencies I have worked before going into my own private practice, I was taught to drill into clients that they can not drink or use drugs no matter where they are in their usage. I found that by doing this, I was faced with a lot of resistance and close-minded clients who would only put in their time in treatment to satisfy the courts and end their current legal problems due to their use. By learning Dr. Glasser's Choice Theory, I have since found that utilizing his concepts that clients will see the need to stop their use on their own without someone else demanding or trying to control them to get them to stop. When someone sees a need for change and it is their choice to make the change, the transition to effect change meets with less resistance.

These concepts work just as effectively in our relationships with others as they do with substance dependence. In fact, they are just as effective in substance dependence as they are in all other so-called mental illness problems found in the DSM-IV. When we are unhappy, we can be pretty creative in our behaviors to compensate for not getting our basic needs met.

All of my clients over the years who have asked for help with their life came with the same problem: They were unhappy. Why were they unhappy? Because someone in their life was not behaving the way that they wanted them to behave. And it may even have been themselves. They were not having happy relationships with the important people in their life.

Just take a moment to look at all of the past unhappiness you may have had or are currently having. Unless you are unhappy about living in poverty stricken or war torn area, you are most likely unhappy because of the behavior of someone else. And you found over the years that when you can't control them and get them to do what you want them to do, you may have used drugs or alcohol to feel better at the time of your unhappiness. Drugs and alcohol are tools that you can no longer use to deal with your unhappiness. All they are doing for you now is causing you to experience more unhappiness.

Let go of the things that you can not control and get in touch with what you can control . . . yourself. Ask for the help of others. This is something that you won't be able to do by yourself. You need friends, a sponsor, another recovering person, a "normie," (a successful and happy person who has never used or abused), and if religious, God or Higher Power, in your life. These are your new tools. Use them, often. They work.

What If I Relapse?

I'd be surprised if you didn't. Most addicts/alcoholics do relapse. But that doesn't mean you have to be one of them. And if you are, then simply start over. I must have relapsed several dozen times when I quit smoking. I relapsed once when drinking. The point is, don't give up. If you slip, don't beat yourself up. You've been doing a pretty good job of doing that for the last several years. Just get back on your plan.

The relapse isn't when you drink or use anyway. It's when you start thinking about drinking or using. And what are the two components of Total Behavior that we have direct control? . . . Our thinking and our acting. Change your thoughts and change how you behave. You will always have two choices: To do one thing (drink or use) or to do something totally different than what you have been doing (not drink or use).

One choice will not make any changes in your life than what you've been doing. Drinking/using has brought you unhappiness due to the loss of meaningful relationships in your life. Drinking/using has also taken a toll on your health as well. Your other choice to not drink/use will only lead to longer abstinence and sobriety so that you can rebuild and acquire the relationships that you need that will bring you health and happiness. Don't ever give up no matter how many times you may relapse. Don't pile on more shame and guilt if you do relapse.

It's OK to mess up. You're human. None of us are perfect. Striving for perfection is one of the leading causes of why people lay on the analyst's couch.

Controlling Urges & Emotions

I have always been very interested in animal behavior and looking for similarities between humans and animals. Long before I ever became a therapist, I would contend that the behavior of peoples' pets was due in part by the behavior of the pet's owner. It wasn't until Cesar Millan, the Dog Whisperer, came along that I was able to put it all together. Cesar had convinced me that dogs, a pack (social) animal like humans, are not people yet so many people treat their dogs as humans and use human psychology to correct their behavior . . .ineffectively. As Cesar has said, we must see dogs as: 1. Animals, 2. Species, 3. Breed, and 4. Name. Instead, we have a tendency to see them as we see other humans: 1. Name, 2. Breed, and 3. Species. We forget about the "animal" part because we don't see our fellow humans as animals, even though we really are. Below is the view of animals that we need to maintain in order to live happily and successfully with them.

1. Animal
2. Dog
3. Boxer
4. Sarah

Instead, we tend to see our pets as we see humans:

1. Bubba
2. Caucasian, or Asian, or Black, or Native American, etc.
3. Human

With this type of view, we then tend to treat the pet more like a human than an animal and attempt to use rationalization and reasoning with them to get them to do what we want them to do with disastrous results.

After watching several of Cesar's shows, it became apparent to me that people psychology can not possibly work on dogs yet dog psychology can be simply utilized with humans, although I don't advise it. Dog psychology is a psychology of dominance. Dominance is natural and healthy in the animal world but not in the human animal world. The dog pack leader exerts his dominance over the remaining pack members and the human utilizes dominance (even if it is calm and assertive) over the dog(s).

Besides the obvious that we do not look like dogs, we have other differences as well. Dogs live only in The Now, in the present. They don't live in the past (although they can be conditioned from the past) nor do they live or are they capable of seeing into the future. We humans, on the other hand, live in the past, the now, and the future. This is what makes us so complex over other animals. We can rationalize. While some animals have the capacity to reason on small scales, humans can reason far and wide.

The key to Cesar Millan's work is that when a dog's mind begins to stray to other things, all in the now, Cesar brings them back to the mind set of where they were before they mentally wandered off. Outside stimuli is the greatest detractor that keeps humans and animals from staying "in the zone."

Some of the things dogs do to get out of the zone when they are being walked are:

1. Sniffing bushes and trees and then peeing to leave their own territory scent.
2. Sniffing the ground to see what has been ahead of them.

3. Passing cars or trucks leading to cowering or running and chasing.

4. Passing kids on bikes and skateboards leading to chasing them.

5. Dogs being walked by other owners leading to attacks.

6. Dogs behind fences that bark and challenge.

7. Fear of other people and things.

8. Protection of owner and owner's property

9. Aggression towards other people.

10. Chasing one's tail and spinning for hours.

11. Aggression towards other living things such as squirrels, cats, birds, etc.

With a slight nudge of the foot, a short jab at the neck with a hand resembling a mouth with teeth, a jerk upward on a leash, or a snap of a finger with his signatory "shhh" is sufficient to bring the animal back into the zone. Those of you who have seen his show know exactly what I am describing and how successful these techniques are.

Like dogs, we humans are social pack animals. In all groups, human or dog, there will always be a pack leader. If no one takes the role, eventually someone in the pack will. If you are not a pack leader with your dog, your dog will become the pack leader in your household and begin doing all of the things that you don't want them to do.

When Cesar meets with the dog owners, he does not acknowledge the dog with eye contact or any greeting whatsoever. The first thing that Cesar does is to get to know the owners, assess their behavior when their dog behaves in a way that is disapproving, and then he "rehabilitates the dog and trains people." Once he shows the owners what they are doing, or what they are not doing, the dog begins to change its behavior . . . usually in 10 minutes or less. Granted, some cases take longer.

The correction for Cesar is to show the dog owners how to become the pack leader, claim the owner's space, claim the owner's ownership of the home and its furnishings, and with calm assertiveness, let the dog know what is acceptable and what is not acceptable. He does this by exercise, discipline, and affection . . . in that order. But it is still dominance and not a behavior that is generally tolerated by other humans.

While watching the National Geographic channel one evening, a program came on showing how humans have engineered the species and behavior of dogs to suit the needs of humans and that 80% of all dog breeds today did not exit 150 years ago. The program went on to show a bull dog who was chasing his tail and spinning in circles until it would stop due to fatigue. The narrator stated that the dog had a (human) mental illness of obsessive compulsive disorder and would eventually need to be put down.

Like so many people who believe that some behaviors or mental illnesses, the narrator is not aware of two things: 1.) There is no pathology to Obsessive Compulsive Behavior and there are no laboratory findings to show the existence of such an "illness." 2.) Cesar Millan cured several dogs on his show with the same behavior of chasing their tails until collapse and had done so in only a few minutes. How? By exercise (walking and taking the role of pack leader), discipline (keeping the dog in his current acceptable mind-set), and reward (no stress, relaxation, and affection). So much for having a "mental illness" and the need to be put down.

One evening, just before Thanksgiving, one of my group clients approached me to tell me that he was having difficulty with his cravings for alcohol especially with the upcoming holiday. I then gave him my standard speech about what to do to control cravings:

They don't last long so just hold on for about 10 or 12 minutes and they'll go away. Get yourself to an A.A. meeting as soon as you have cravings. Call your sponsor. If you don't have one, get one. Exercise. Run around the block or do something strenuous for about ten minutes. Find something else to do to occupy your thoughts, etc., etc.

After the client left, I began to think to myself: I've been saying this to clients for years and I don't buy it myself. So why should I think my clients will buy it and put it to use. They need to do something that will put their thoughts back into "the zone" of not thinking about drinking or using.

And then it dawned on me. Why not use some of Cesar's techniques to get thoughts back into the zone? People psychology won't work on dogs but dog psychology can work on people.

I went to group the next night and mixed Choice Theory with Cesar Millan's techniques. I explained to them that we are social pack animals just like dogs. I then showed them that our Quality World was our zone . . . those things that bring us happiness and when the real world images don't match our quality world images, we get frustrated. I then referred to the 5 basic needs and how any shortage in these areas will also cause frustration. Any time we choose to frustrate, we get "out of the zone" and lose our happiness. I explained that any unwanted negative emotion could be controlled.

I asked the group to take the next two days to do what Cesar does to stop a dog from unwanted behavior: He snaps his finger and firmly says "shhh" while taking a stance of calm assertiveness. Of course, they all laughed at me but agreed to give it a try. Two days later, I asked to see the hands of those who had use the exercise more than once. Several hands went up and each told their story of how it worked for them.

We then began to talk about all of the many distractions we might experience that would move us from our happy or complacent zone to unhappy frustration and unwanted emotions. Of course drugs and alcohol were at the top of the list for cravings. Other distractions were the seven deadly habits of others when utilized on us; the behavior of someone else that we disapproved of; disappointments when things don't go the way we expect or want.

So then the group agreed to utilize it for any and all unwanted emotions and cravings for alcohol and drugs. The results were amazing. All the group members stated that they used it and that it had been effective means to put them back into the happiness or neutral zone and took them out of the unwanted emotions and cravings.

There was, however, some concern about the actual practice. Many clients stated that they felt uncomfortable doing the finger snap and "shhh" while in the presence of others. I agreed and stated that this practice should be done alone and not used especially in the presence of someone else whom you might be involved with in a heated argument. Snapping the finger and saying "shhh" in front of them would be taken as dominance and aggression towards the other person instead of them understanding that you were using it for your own benefit.

The group then decided that they could do it silently in their own mind whenever needed. So this became the exercise. Now comes the discipline: You must use this exercise on a regular basis to the point where it becomes natural and you don't have to think about doing it. Instead of affection, you will receive a reward of achieving and maintaining more happiness than you have been accustomed to for the last several years of your life. You will become the pack leader of your emotions that will allow you to stay in the now and make better choices instead of reacting emotionally.

Any time you feel the urge to use or drink, take (Act) an assertive and dominant stance. Admit that what you are feeling is something that you don't want to feel that will lead to negative consequences. Visualize your craving as an animal or whatever creature you want to associate it with. Take one step forward while snapping your finger at it and loudly demanding, "SHHH!" Do it as often as necessary and watch the urge cower and be submissive.

Triggers

Assignment Five: Dealing with Triggers.

What are some of those things that make you reach into your tool kit for your alcohol or drug? Whatever they are, it started for some specific reasons and later graduated into still other reasons. Something from the real world is not matching your values or images inside your quality world.

Do you ever want to drink or use a drug because you feel shy, inferior, or unworthy when around others and when you do drink or drug, you don't give a damn about those thoughts or feelings?

Do you ever want to drink or use a drug because you feel more outgoing, friendly, or even more intelligent when you do?

Do you ever want to drink or use a drug because you feel tense or nervous and you want to calm down or relax?

Do you ever want to drink or use a drug to deal with unwanted feelings such as disappointment, sadness, shame, guilt, or anger?

Do you ever want to drink or use a drug to feel you are in a better frame of mind than you would be if not drinking or using?

Do you ever want to drink or use a drug when someone else uses the seven deadly habits of criticizing, blaming, complaining, threatening, punishing, nagging, and bribing you?

Do you ever want to drink or use a drug when a marriage or relationship ends?

Do you ever want to drink the minute a football or baseball game comes on TV?

Do you ever want to drink or use a drug after a quarrel with someone important to you or if the boss gives you a hard time?

Do you ever want to drink or use a drug if you feel like a loser?

Do you ever want to drink or use a drug if you are having financial problems?

Do you ever want to drink or use a drug when someone in your life is behaving in a way that you disapprove of?

Here's the general question that will encompass all of the reasons you may drink or use a drug: Do you ever want to drink or use a drug if there is a gap between what you want and what you have?

The triggers above are all the result of how you see yourself and how you really want to be. The images of what you want and what you don't have create frustration. You want happiness and you don't have it. When you compare the image of quality world and the image doesn't match your perceived world, you see two distinctly different images. What you've been doing, so far, to deal with these opposing images is to either drink or use drugs. Doing so, you no longer feel the frustration of the images that don't match as well as, you just don't give a damn. So while you don't care and while your frustration is gone, your lack of caring and your frustration will return as soon as you sober up. Since this method doesn't seem to work in helping the images to match, the only thing your behavior has done is to continually deal with it by staying drunk or high to ignore it.

So what do you think you could do make the image you have of yourself in your perceived world match the image of yourself in the real world? Who has the power to change the image of yourself in the perceived world? It is certainly not I. Only you. Are you getting this? This is some important stuff. No one can make you stop drinking or using except you. No one can change the person you want to be in your quality world to match the image in the perceived world except yourself.

The above questions may have been why you began drinking on a regular basis but there are other reasons for drinking or using a drug that I haven't asked yet.

Do you ever want to drink or use a drug because if you don't, your hands shake?

Do you ever want to drink or use a drug because if you don't, you feel sick or nauseous?

Do you ever want to drink or use a drug because if you don't, you ache from head to foot . . . and even your hair hurts?

Do you ever want to drink or use a drug because if you don't, you will throw up or have a seizure?

Do you ever want to drink or use a drug because if you don't, you will have a panic attack, see or hear things, or become paranoid?

How many of those questions did you answer in the affirmative? A "yes" response to any of those questions requires you to seek medical detox for your own health and welfare. Don't try to quit drinking or using without medical supervision. They have meds to help you get through the really rough parts that might end up in death.

If you have a leaky water pipe in your home, do you fix it with chewing gum, duct tape, nail polish, or do you replace the pipe?

If you have a low tire, do you continue to drive on it by continually filling it with air, or do you get it fixed or replace it?

Now for some outrageous questions:

Do you continue to drink or use even after all of your family, friends, spouse, children, or employer have taken you out of their quality world?

Do you continue to drink or use even though a doctor has told you to quit because of you health?

Do you continue to drink or use even though you can't afford to do so?

Do you continue to drink or use even though you have lost jobs because of it?

Do you continue to drink or use even though you have been hospitalized or have a serious physical or emotional condition as a result of your drinking or using?

Do you continue to drink or use drugs even though you have been arrested for drinking or using or spent time in jail or prison because of drinking or drug use?

A "yes" response to any one of the many questions above would indicate that you most definitely have a problem with alcohol or drugs or both. None of the above behaviors are indicative of happy and healthy people. They are the behaviors of those who are unhappy and only doing their best to find happiness.

If you are alone and have lost all of your family and friends, they you have detached from a very important genetic need of love and belonging and you will need to re-attach to those people who are important people in your life.

To simplify this chapter on triggers or cravings to drink or to use, triggers are no more than your mind's reaction of unhappiness in your life and your habit of going to the tool box to pull out your favorite drug or drink to deal with it. Urges to drink or to use come and go. Call your sponsor in A.A., C.A. or N.A if you have been using the 12 step program. Go to a meeting!!! Call a friend and talk. Exercise. Drink water or tea. Use the Cesar Millan approach to your triggers. Deal with them as you would an unruly dog: With calm assertiveness. Visualize whatever it is that is causing you to react to your emotions and/or physiology as a mean dog . . . snarling and threatening you with growls and barking. Point to it, take one step forward, and command it to "SHHHH!"

The topic here is not dealing with your withdrawals. We are more concerned about those times when you get it in your head that you want to drink or use because of something that happened or something you were doing reminded of your past use and you have an urge to use or drink at this moment. These urges are not generally long lasting. Fight them for 10 minutes or so and they will go away. The more you do this the more you will overcome them in the future. The rain will fall on everyone at one time or another. It isn't so much as what happens to you in life as it is how you DEAL with what happens to you in life. Your tool kit needs some additional and effective tools.

The best way to overcome your triggers is to talk about them. You can't talk about them unless you have some people in your life that you can talk to. Can you see how important it is to have meaningful and non-obligatory relationships in your life?

Simply stated: Your triggers are the stressors you have in your life. In the past, you always relied on your drug or alcohol to deal with them. Part of recovery from addiction is the process of learning new and better ways to deal with your stressors than resorting to drugs or alcohol.

You Can't Make Me

You're right. And I don't want to "make" you. You are the only one who can put any changes into place in your life. My purpose in putting my thoughts into words in this book is only to take the position of someone on the outside to assist you in finding other possible means that make sense to you to try and see if you like the outcome.

I can't help but notice how many treatment agencies discharge the clients who relapse. What kind of help is that to be giving them? If someone is blatantly refusing to make any effort to overcome their addiction, someone else needs to work a little harder at giving the client options to make his life better? I can hear you yelling at me right now: "Hey Rice, isn't that External Control?" In a sense, yes, it is. It's trying to get someone to do something that they don't want to do. But by utilizing Reality Therapy and Choice Theory, the process is offered to the client in a manner that is not forcing them to make changes. If the client is telling you that he really wants to be happier and alcohol or drug free, how is that making him/her do what they don't want to do?

Choice Theory and Reality Therapy give clients alternatives that clients may want to try . . . things that they haven't done before that have a good chance of enriching the client's life. And if the client continues to refuse to make any life-enhancing behaviors after coming up with several options, then the therapist has choices to make: Not to give up or admit there is nothing that that therapist can do for the client at this time. The idea is for the client to come up with different behaviors and thoughts, not for the therapist to come up with them. It has been my experience that if the client doesn't do any of the things that he said he would do, then he didn't want to do them in the first place and other alternatives will need to be discovered. This is why it is important to get a commitment out of the client to see just how willing s/he is to follow through and begin to make some changes in their life.

I don't know any addict or alcoholic who wants to continue their life of addiction. Down deep, they want to get back to being happy. If what they have been doing is the cause of all of their unhappiness, what are some things that they might want to do that they haven't tried that will bring them the happiness that they want? They have discovered a tool in the form of alcohol or drugs that covers up their unhappiness and cures nothing. And while it is covering up their unhappiness, they are losing all of the people in their life that will bring them happiness . . . meaningful relationships.

Being defiant in treatment is just a continuation of behavior that the client has been doing for years. Defiance or reluctance to make changes has the effect of getting not only the people they don't like out of their life, it also gets rid of the people that they do like in their life. They are choosing behaviors that they see as meeting their basic needs of survival, freedom, and power. What they fail to perceive is how these behaviors are what are causing them all of their unhappiness.

Again, the importance of self-evaluation can not be overestimated.

What do happy and successful people do that you aren't doing?

What do happy and successful people have that you don't have?

If what you have been doing isn't working, why continue to do it?

Rearrange Your Quality World

Recently you have had the image of alcohol or your drug of choice in your quality world. You are the only person who can take that value and image out of your quality world. Replace them with images of you being a happy person who has friends who care for and love you and those whom you love and care for. Replace the drugs and alcohol with love, happiness, accomplishment, and peace of mind.

If you were in possession of the above qualities, how would you look differently than the way you look right now? Would you see a happier person or not? What are some of the things that you can do in order to make those images match your real world image of yourself? What do you see other happy, healthy, and successful people doing that you have not been doing?

They are taking responsibility of their own life and making positive choices that fulfill their life. They don't make good choices all the time. They make poor choices just like you. But they don't give up. They realize when something is not working for them and they find other choices. Over the years they have found out what works and what doesn't work. Do they have all of the tools one can have? No. They are still learning just like you will be doing. The only difference is that they got a head start on collecting their tools. But don't concern yourself with them. Concern yourself only with you and the tools that you need to get you the desired results you want in your life.

Stop using rocks, pliers, screwdrivers, and shoes to hammer a nail and get a hammer. You'll be amazed at how easier it is to get the job done when you have the right tool.

Behavior Review

Let's take a look at all the things we must come to understand and know in order for us to become clean and sober and work towards recovery and acquire happiness in our lives.

1. The ONLY person we can control in our lives is our self.
2. External Control and the Seven Deadly habits (Criticizing, blaming, complaining, nagging, threatening, punishing, bribing/rewarding) are a primary cause of our conflict with others. Either someone is using them on you and/or you are using them on others. STOP USING THE SEVEN DEADLY HABITS. When others use them on you, stop reacting the way you have been when they do so. The leading cause of your unhappiness is your failure to maintain a meaningful relationship with those whom you want to have meaningful relationships.
3. ALL OF YOUR BEHAVIORS ARE CHOSEN. Start taking responsibility for your happiness as well as you unhappiness. Start taking responsibility for your sobriety.
4. All of your behavior serves to meet one or more of the five genetic needs of
    a. Survival
    b. Love & Belonging
    c. Power
    d. Freedom
    e. Fun

All of the behavior of others serves to meet one or more of their five genetic needs as well.

5. You possess pictures or images as well as values of those things that are important to you . . . those things that bring you happiness. Addicts and Alcoholics have the

image of their drug of choice in their quality world as well as other things that they believe bring them happiness. You are the only one who can put in or take out any of those images. No one else can do it for you. Usually, when you take something out, you replace it with something else.

6. When those things that we perceive in the real world do not match the images you have in your quality world, you begin to do things in an effort to control the situation by making the two images match. The mind can be very creative when striving to meet this goal. Find new ways instead of alcohol/drugs.

7. Alcohol and drugs fool your brain into thinking that you are happy by affecting the pleasure centers of your brain. In reality, you are only drugging your brain and fooling yourself into thinking that whatever has been bothering you has been resolved . . . until you sober up and discover that the problem is still there.

8. Your total behavior consists of thinking, feeling, physiology, and action. Of those four components, you can directly control two of them: Thoughts and Actions. Controlling these two components will lead to indirect control of your emotions and physiology. Therefore, when faced with conflict:

    1. Change what you want and/or

    2. Change how you react when you don't get what you want.

Once you have internalized this information and use it to your advantage, you can now begin to apply it not only in your personal relationships with others but with yourself, as well . . . specifically . . . treating your addictions and behaviors.

Addiction Review

1. You have a problem with drugs or alcohol and have come to admit it and accept it.

2. Your pre-addiction use of alcohol/drugs was a choice. You continued to drink/use until your body and mind became dependent upon it. Now **you have a choice to continue to drink/use or not drink/use.**

3. Re-read the chapter on Getting Started. Come to the unquestionable conclusion that what you have been doing with drugs/alcohol has been causing you most, if not all, of your happiness and problems in your life. Nothing will change in your life if you don't start making changes. **See the need**. You will experience withdrawal symptoms emotionally, psychologically, and physically. Refer to the chapter on what to expect when you quit when it comes to dealing with them. Fight the withdrawals. Don't allow them to overpower your thinking that leads to relapse. They won't last forever. You can rise above them but only through dogged determination and suffering through them. Get medical help if necessary.

4. Make new acquaintances of those who no longer drink/use by going to A.A. meetings or other self-help support groups. Make new acquaintances with those who have NEVER had a problem with drugs or alcohol. Learn how they think. Observer how they live. Develop meaningful and non-obligatory relationships.

5. STAY IN THE NOW. Avoid going back into your past to open up old hurts or to attempt to control something that has already happened. You can't change the past. You can only control now and tomorrow. Do you choose to be happy or miserable in the now? Each day that you go without a drink or a drug is one more day to add to your sobriety and recovery. Continue to stay in the now and you will soon not have to think about it. You'll just do it. Then you can claim your recovery and happiness.

6. Know what your triggers are. Discover new and different ways to deal with them than reaching for your favorite drug or alcoholic drink. Your cravings and triggers are short lived. Triggers may occur often but they don't last long.

All of the above reviews are simply stated actions or behaviors that you have a choice to use or not use. No matter what, it still always comes down to CHOICES. You can't follow a map to a treasure unless you follow each direction on the map. To leave any direction out will lead to losing your way towards your quest.

Quite often, clients will approach me and ask what it is that they can do when dealing with their urges to drink/use, or with dealing with their "using dreams." As I begin to explore with them all of the things they need to be doing, it is always discovered that they are not doing one or more of the steps to reach their recovery. They are picking and choosing what it is they are willing to do and leaving out those things that they don't want to do and then complain that it isn't working for them.

You may have to read this book several times or, at least, refer to specific chapters for re-reading in order to acquire full knowledge and understanding of what it is you are omitting or not doing that is leading to your difficulty in maintaining sobriety and recovery. If you follow the steps as well as become active in A.A. or some other support group, you should have no difficulty reaching your goal.

Once you acquire happiness, you will no longer need to put anything into your body to make you feel better about yourself or your life. I have never had a client call me to make an appointment to see me because they were so damn happy, they couldn't stand it. I have never seen a truly happy person rely on drugs or alcohol to get through the day or through life. I have never seen a person maintain success or happiness while consistently relying on drugs or alcohol. In fact, I have observed them losing all that they ever had before they became dependent. And more times than not, I have seen happiness and success lost just as soon as one achieved it due to the use of drugs or alcohol.

If nothing changes, nothing changes. If your life is not where you want it to be; if you're tired of wondering why others seem to be happier or more successful than you; if you never seem to have enough money; if all or most of the important people in your life no longer have anything to do with you, if your health is suffering, if you're severely depressed, get rid of your drug or alcohol habit. And while you are maintaining a drug-free life, refuse to take any other drugs such as any antidepressants, Ritilan®, Adderal®, or anxiety meds that any doctor or psychiatrist may prescribe. If you're a drug addict, the drugs I listed are no more than using ecstasy, cocaine, or other drugs that affect your behavior with no curative powers.

If you recall, the image of a car was utilized to describe Total Behavior: The front wheels represent thoughts and actions while the rear wheels represent emotions and physiology. Since we can only directly control our thoughts and actions, the image of the steering wheel was attached to those wheels.

Using drugs or alcohol causes one to place drug affected emotions over intellect and in doing so, s/he tries to steer the car with the steering wheel attached to the rear wheels. This is a method doomed for failure.

Are you familiar with those flatbed carts you can find at the big box hardware stores? There is a tall bar about chest high to grab in order to pull the cart. Notice I said "pull." The wheels that move right or left on this cart are on the rear of the cart. If you were to try and push this cart, you would be bumping into every person and item in the store. The only way to control this cart is to pull it and not push it. You successfully steer by controlling the wheels that are movable. The same principal goes for the grocery cart at your local supermarket. The wheels on a grocery cart that move right or left are on the front, not the back. Consequently, you push the cart and don't pull it.

Those who steer their life via the wheels of emotions and physiology will find themselves bumping into all sorts of things and crashing into anything that gets close to them. If you attempt to walk a straight line backwards, you will find it very difficult to do as opposed to walking a straight line forward. Control your life with the wheels that you can directly control. It's your choice.

About the Author

Michael Rice is a certified Reality and Choice Theory Therapist and a licensed alcohol and drug therapist living in Mesa, Arizona. He has been in private practice, treating over 250 alcohol and drug abusers and addicts a year for the last 15 years. Mr. Rice considers himself to be a "happiness teacher" rather than a therapist. "I treat some so-called mental illness conditions not as a mental illness, but merely as someone who is unhappy. They are unhappy because of an unsatisfying relationship with someone important to them in their lives in which they want to have a satisfying relationship. Besides that, since when is drug and alcohol addiction or abuse a mental illness?"

Mike contends that a great deal of what is being called "mental illness" is no more than people who are creatively trying to get their basic needs met. He also contends that practically every mental illness listed in the DSM IV has no pathology and this fact is even admitted to by the authors of the book under Associated Laboratory Findings for each illness classification. In other words, a person is diagnosed as mentally ill because someone else said they were, and there is no test or physical examination that can prove or substantiate it. "How many people would have surgery or take medication simply because someone else said it was needed even though no testing had been done and there was nothing to prove the illness existed?"

Mike speaks to various groups of people about Choice Theory and how it can change their personal and business life to one of happiness without the need for medication and how to resolve conflict with the important people in one's life.

Reference Listing

- Geiwitz, James. *Psychology: Looking at Ourselves.* Boston, MA: Little, Brown & Company 1976.
- Glasser, William and Glasser, Carleen. *Getting Together and Staying Together.* New York: Harper Collins Publishing, Inc. 1995.
- Glasser, William. *Choice Theory: A New Psychology of Personal Freedom.* New York: Harper Collins Publishers, Inc. 1998.
- Glasser, William. *Counseling With Choice Theory; The New Reality Therapy.* New York: Harper Collins Publishers, Inc. 2000.
- Glasser, William. *Warning: Psychology Can Be Hazardous to Your Mental Health.* New York: Harper Collins Publishers, Inc. 2003.
- Glasser, William; Glasser, Carleen. *Eight Lessons for a Happier Marriage.* New York: Harper Collins Publishers, Inc. 2007.
- Hendrix, Harville. *Getting the Love Your Want: A Guide for Couples.* New York: Harper and Row 1990.
- Maslow, Abraham. *Motivation and Personality* New York: Harper, 1954.
- NIDA Infofacts: *Cigarettes and Other Tobacco Products.* (2006) http://www.NIDA.nih.gov/Infofacts/tobacco.html
- The Johari Window (2007) http://www.12manage.com/methods_luft_ingham_j ohari_window.html
- Wubbolding, Robert E. *Reality Therapy for the 21st Century.* Philadelphia, PA: Brunner-Routledge 2000.

(This page intentionally left blank)

Made in the USA
Lexington, KY
17 March 2011